CW00665985

MY

THAI

COOKBOOK

Thai Food****

is electrifying and **invigorating** and makes the tongue tingle with excitement. You remember the first time you tasted it. When you try the real stuff, you are soon hooked. You are literally craving more and more amazing flavors. Chile is actually addictive and makes you feel good when you eat it, so maybe this is the reason why.

The myth of Thai cooking is that its exotic secrets are hard to master and out of reach to the home cook. We instead settle for cheap takeout, which seemed like a good idea at the time but is often disappointing.

Cooking really good authentic Thai food is actually relatively easy. There is a bit of prep to do, but the cooking process is not hard. What is vital is getting a balance of taste. In Thailand this is called "ROT CHART," where flavors are enhanced and defined. Rot – meaning "taste" and chart meaning "proper, unified, balanced" – is the ultimate goal of Thai cooking.

In Thai cooking there are four main groups of taste – hot, sweet, sour, and salt. HOT includes pepper and spices, represented by fresh and dried chile, whole and ground pepper, dried and fresh spices, ginger, garlic, galangal, and turmeric. The chemical opposite of hot is SWEET, which comes from sugar, palm sugar, fruit or honey as well as toasted coconut or coconut cream. More complex sweet elements are shrimp or seafood like crab, or roasted pork or duck. Lime and lemon juice and rice vinegar are SOUR, as are the complex characteristics of tamarind, lemongrass, and lime leaves. The SALT in Thai cooking comes from fish sauce, soy sauce, savory toasted nuts, salted smoked fish, and dried shrimp.

All of these tastes must be in balance in every mouthful and in every dish. The key to mastering this balance of flavors is by tasting your food throughout the cooking process. This sounds simple, doesn't it? However, most cooks do not do it often enough. Take a piece of watermelon and eat it, then squeeze some lime and taste it again – the watermelon's flavor much more exciting. Season again with salt and lime and taste – now things are beginning to heat up. Finally, sprinkle a pinch of red pepper flakes or ground black pepper on the watermelon. With salt and lime you have created extraordinary food that sparks a fireworks display on your taste buds. This is Thai cooking. Once tried, there is no turning back.

MY THAI COOKBOOK takes your taste buds on a culinary adventure, from classic well-known staples to authentic dishes that only the more intrepid Thai food fanatics have really experienced. These recipes come from vibrant street-food markets and exotic coastal backdrops and ancient royal palaces. What ties them all together, however, is that their mystique has been unveiled to reveal some truly delicious healthy food that is easy to make, impressive to serve, and perfect for today's cooks.

TOP 12 STAR
Experiences in Thailand

1. Take your elephant for a river bath in the Northern Jungle of Chang Mai and sample some *Kai Yang*, Isaan-style chicken with black pepper and lemongrass.

2. Have an authentic massage in the Thai massage school at Wat Pho, the temple of the reclining Buddha in Bangkok. Eat Thai fish cakes or banana fritters from one of the stalls outside the temple.

3. Sip a Mai Thai cocktail overlooking the beach in Phuket. Admire the view and enjoy some turmeric-grilled fish or a bowl of spice-fried squid.

4. Have a singha beer at a Thai kickboxing competition. Get a real kick with a Thai beef stir-fry with chile and onion relish.

5. Eat street food while being gracefully rowed around the historic floating markets of Amphawa. Why not try a hot and sour green papaya salad to really feel at home.

6. Eat a jungle curry, looking out over the jungle. Originating from northern Thailand, these curries are fiery and have no coconut cream. They were historically made with wild boar. If you can't stand the heat and you want something a bit less hot, then how about a red curry with caramelized chicken?

7. Buy a knockoff designer bag or watch for a few dollars in a night market while enjoying some banana and coconut pancakes or sweet and crispy pork spare ribs.

8. Take a slow ride in a cyclo to experience the crazy atmosphere in Bangkok. Why not eat some Hakka-style fried pork noodles?

9. Find your own ideal beach. Don't bother going with all the other tourists to visit Maya Bay, the film set from *The Beach*. Instead, find your own piece of paradise. Or simply drink a pineapple mint ginger crush and close your eyes and dream.

10. Take part in a hands-on Thai cooking class in a royal palace and learn how to make spicy ocean broth with herbed fish cakes.

11. Lay in an island hammock sipping a freshly picked young coconut. Why not try the coconut cream pudding – simple and exotic – just like a Thai island hammock.

12. Pick your own spices in a pepper plantation while cycling around the picturesque countryside, then enjoy some crispy fried whitebait with Thai spices or fragrant chicken wings with galangal.

CHANG MAI
Kai yang (Isaan-style chicken with lemongrass & black pepper)

NIGHT MARKET
Banana & coconut pancakes

NORTHERN JUNGLE
Jungle curry

PEPPER PLANTATION
Crispy fried whitebait with Thai spices

ROYAL PALACE BANGKOK
Spicy ocean broth with herbed fish cakes

BANGKOK

TEMPLE OF THE RECLINING BUDDHA
Thai fish cakes

FLOATING MARKETS OF AMPHAWA
Hot and sour green papaya salad

BANGKOK CYCLO
Hakka-style fried pork noodles

ISLAND LIFE
Coconut cream pudding

PHUKET
Mai Thai cocktail & spice fried squid

BEACH PARADISE
Pineapple mint ginger crush

Ingredients
for Thai Cooking

Fresh Ingredients, Nuts & Seeds

LEMONGRASS

Lemongrass imparts all the citrus flavors of lemon and lime but without the acidity and bitterness. When using, remove all the tough outer leaves. Buy fresh stems that are bulbous at the bottom and near white in color. Use a sharp knife to finely slice the stems into thin slivers. Lemongrass can be eaten raw in salads and as a garnish or puréed and cooked in curry pastes. You can also cut it into thin slices, freeze it, and use it directly from the freezer.

GINGER

Ginger has extraordinary culinary and medicinal value. When buying, make sure you choose plump young pieces. The skin and peelings can be crushed and puréed for soups and curry pastes. The flesh can be sliced and eaten raw in salads or as a garnish.

CILANTRO ROOTS

These sound exotic but are really as simple as they sound – the roots at the bottom of a bunch of cilantro. If you are growing your own cilantro, instead of cutting off the bunch, pull the whole thing out like a bunch of carrots. The roots provide an intense flavor when used in pastes, marinades, and sauces. If the roots are not available, use the lower part of the stems instead and finely chop them. They can be bought in bags in good Asian stores. The roots can be finely chopped or ground and eaten raw or cooked.

THAI BASIL

Thai basil has shiny dark green leaves that are more spear shaped that Western basil and often have a purple tinge. This basil has a strong lemony star anise/aniseed taste, which is very distinctive. Try and find it fresh where possible as dried or frozen is not as good. It is available from Asian stores, but use some fragrant Western basil if you can't find any.

LIME LEAVES

These are the dark shiny leaves from the kaffir lime tree. They have the most amazing heady aroma when broken or torn and impart an extraordinary perfume and fragrance. You can buy them dry, however if you freeze them from fresh, they keep their color and flavor. If not available, use fresh lime zest instead as it provides all the citrus aroma and taste without any of the acidity. To shred the lime leaves, trim the raised stem on the underside of the leaf, tightly roll the leaves into a cigar shape and cut across in very thin slices to produce a fine shred.

CHILES

The use of chile is important in Thai cooking as it provides the heat to balance the other flavors. Chiles vary in strength so always taste a little before you add to your dish. It is much easier to increase the heat than try and take it away from your food. The small bird's-eye chiles are the hottest. Dried chile is also much hotter than fresh chile. A number of the recipes call for seeded and finely chopped long red chiles – this is a way of you having a bit more control of the heat content. With a complete balance of taste the opposite of peppery hot is sweet. If your dish is too hot, temper it with something sweet or neutral such as coconut cream, palm sugar, or fruit.

GARLIC

Garlic is used a lot in Thai cooking, although it is possible to make Thai cuisine without it. If you want to avoid using garlic, you can use more ginger, cilantro roots, and chile instead. When garlic is used in a sauce or paste it will be raw. For this reason a mortar and pestle are essential in Thai cooking. The garlic cloves can be crushed with a little salt so that you don't have big chunks in a sauce. Raw garlic is peppery hot, but when it is cooked it becomes sweet and rich tasting.

BLANCHED SKINLESS PEANUTS

Toasted peanuts are used in many different Thai dishes. You can buy unsalted peanuts either with or without the skin from Asian stores. Toast peanuts over a moderate heat in a frying pan or in a moderate oven until they are golden brown. Do not let them become too dark as they will be bitter. Let cool, then crush or chop them. Always check if anyone has a peanut allergy before serving.

CASHEW NUTS

Buy raw unsalted cashew nuts. Toast until golden brown. If you are preparing Thai food for someone who has a nut allergy, you can use toasted rice to form the nutty texture in the dish instead of nuts (see page 17).

SESAME SEEDS

Seeds provide a much needed texture to Thai dishes. Toast sesame seeds over moderate heat or in the oven until golden brown and crunchy.

Spices

TURMERIC

Turmeric is a root plant related to ginger and can be used fresh in many dishes. However, fresh turmeric is not always readily available, so ground turmeric is used in all the recipes in this book. Turmeric is peppery hot with an aromatic and slightly earthy taste. Turmeric stains easily, and its bright yellow color has been used as a dye for thousands of years. Make sure when you are using it in the kitchen that you only add it to food when it is cooking in a stainless steel pan or bowl. If ground turmeric comes into contact with anything plastic, such as a food-processor bowl or a spatula, it will dye it a deep yellow-orange color. A little ground turmeric goes a long way, but it is essential for curry pastes. The color is warm and welcoming.

CINNAMON

Cinnamon is a warm and generous spice whose flavor evokes memories of Christmas. Available as sticks or ground, it is a delicious addition to your food. Cinnamon is often used in desserts and that is where it is most familiar (try the Roasted Fruits with Thai Aromatic Spices on page 218 or the Banana & Coconut Pancakes on page 214). However, it is also used in Geng Gari Curry Paste (page 226) and Spiced Bavette Steak with Hot & Sour Sauce (page 94). Ground cinnamon responds really well and becomes fragrant and aromatic when it is toasted. Grind your own spices in a small electric spice or coffee grinder, or using a mortar and pestle.

CUMIN SEEDS

Cumin seeds are at their best and most delicious when they are toasted until aromatic, and then ground. This is a spice that is predominantly associated with Indian cooking; however, it is often used in Thai cooking, in particular in curry pastes such as Geng Gari (page 226) and Mussaman (page 228). Toasted cumin provides a delicious three-dimensional depth of flavor when used in roasted duck curry or spice fried squid or grilled meat.

CORIANDER SEEDS

Coriander seeds could not taste more different from fresh cilantro (also known as coriander) or cilantro roots, all of which are used frequently in the Thai kitchen. Always use whole seeds, and crush or grind them yourself, as you will get a much cleaner and more aromatic taste. Ground spices are convenient, but they are often dusty and stale and you do not know when or how they were ground. When you grind your own spices, you get a lot of flavor and a little texture to the grind, which is really important. Like cumin, coriander seeds work well when they are lightly toasted until fragrant, then crushed using a mortar and pestle or ground in an electric spice or coffee grinder.

STAR ANISE

This is a truly amazing spice that has an extraordinary taste. The intense perfume of aniseed is very evocative, when you first smell it in a Thai street-food market or with some roasted pork belly. Simply break the hard spices into a few pieces so that you release the oils and aromatic qualities when it is cooking. You can also grind the spices in a spice grinder for use in spice blends. Star anise is delicious with roasted caramelized meat, such as pork or beef.

PEPPER

Dried black and white pepper are both frequently used whole, finely ground, and coarsely ground. Fresh green peppercorns are also used still on the vine and added to curries and soups to provide a bite. Much of Thai cuisine contains chiles, either fresh or dried, however, it was only after the Portuguese had traveled to South America in the sixteenth century that chiles were introduced to southern Asia and Southeast Asia, including Thailand. Previous to this, black and white pepper was used to create heat along with ingredients such as ginger and garlic.

FIVE-SPICE POWDER

There are numerous spice mix combinations used in Thai cooking and other Southeast Asia cuisines. The mixes are at their best and most fragrant when ground to order from whole spices, then blended. Five-spice powder has both medicinal and culinary importance and is used to season meats and poultry in China, Vietnam, and Thailand. It frequently contains fennel seeds, star anise, cinnamon, cloves, and Sichuan pepper, and has a very distinctive aroma. Once you've made your own blend you'll never look back.

SEN ME NOODLES

SEN LEK NOODLES

STICKY RICE

JASMINE RICE

SEN YAI NOODLES

BASMATI RICE

Pantry Ingredients

SPRING ROLL WRAPPERS

This is paper-thin pastry that is bought pre-rolled in packages. It's available at Asian markets and well-stocked grocery stores. Keep sealed so that pastry layers do not dry out.

RICE NOODLES

There are numerous widths of rice noodles that are bought dried. They need to be soaked in warm water for 20 minutes before using.

SEN MEE are very fine and wiry when dried and are also called rice vermicelli. They are used in spring rolls, soups, stir-fries, and salads.

SEN YAI are broad in width (about ¾–1¼ inches wide) and are also called rice river noodles and rice sticks. When they are bought fresh, they can be quite sticky and will need to be separated. Good for a stir-fry such as Pad Thai Fried Noodles (page 176) where there is lots of sauce.

SEN LEK are a thinner rice noodle (about ⅜ inch in width). They are commonly sold dried and are probably the most widely available. Soak before cooking and they will only take a couple of minutes to cook.

BA MEE noodles are made with egg and rice flour so they are a mid yellow color and are more similar to Italian spaghetti. They are often used for stir-fries and soups.

WUN SEN are very fine, almost translucent in color, and are made with soya flour. They are called cellophane or glass noodles. They will not need a lot of cooking and are great for salads and cold noodle dishes with shrimp and seafood.

THAI STICKY OR GLUTINOUS RICE

This is a particular variety of short-grain rice. It needs to be soaked in cold running water before it is steamed and is often used for desserts.

THAI JASMINE OR FRAGRANT RICE

This is a longer grain rice that is used to accompany curries and is essentially served at every meal in Thai cooking. If you have rice even with a simple sauce it is considered a meal. This is still quite a starchy rice so it does need to be soaked before it is cooked, and it can be cooked in a rice cooker.

BASMATI RICE

Basmati rice is a long-grain Indian rice whose name means fragrant. This type of grain is much less starchy than Thai short-grain rices. It is perfect for making a pilaf and will accompany any Thai curry if you do not have any Thai Jasmine or sticky rice on hand.

Pantry Ingredients

COCONUT MILK & CREAM

This is available in cans from supermarkets and Asian markets. There are lots of options, but I recommend choosing ones that have a Thai label. The liquid inside the can is made up of thinner coconut milk and thicker coconut cream. It can be stirred and used together, or some recipes will call for the two parts to be used at separate points during cooking.

SOY SAUCE

There are two main types of soy sauce. Light soy sauce is light colored, almost clear, and is the more salty of the two. It is used to provide the much needed salty element in Thai cuisine. Dark soy sauce is thicker and stronger tasting and is made richer with the addition of a little molasses. There is also a sweet soy sauce often called ABC sauce, or *kecap manis*, which is thicker and richer and sweeter still. A little goes a long way, so use it sparingly.

BLENDED SESAME OIL

This is mid brown in color and intensely nutty in flavor. Use it sparingly as a little goes a long way. This is another salty, savory, smoky element that adds complexity to a dish and is often used in sauces.

FISH SAUCE

This is the fundamental salty and savory flavoring in Thai and Southeast Asian cuisine. In Thailand it is called *nam pla*, and in Vietnam it is called *nuoc mam*. It is made from salting and fermenting small fish, with fish sauce being the run-off liquid. It can vary in saltiness – the lighter and more golden whiskey-colored it is the better. If it is very dark, then it is older and could be bitter. Fish sauce on its own is not a pleasant experience; however, when combined with lime juice there is a great balance of taste. If you have added too much fish sauce, then add some more lime juice to temper the saltiness.

SHRIMP PASTE

This dark purple paste, also known as Gapi shrimp paste, has a very pungent smell when it is raw (you would be forgiven for thinking that there must be some mistake and how could you possibly add it to your food). When toasted or broiled it loses all its pungency and provides a rich savory taste to a dish. Use sparingly and keep sealed in an airtight container.

OYSTER SAUCE

SESAME OIL

COCONUT MILK

RICE VINEGAR

FISH SAUCE

TAMARIND PASTE

Tamarind is the pulp from the pods of the tamarind tree. It is dark and sticky, like a date, and has an extraordinary taste that is sweet and makes your mouth pucker with sourness. It is high in vitamin C and provides a depth of intensely sour flavor to a dish, especially curries. Tamarind paste is available in jars and tubs in Asian markets. It is also available as a compressed block. To use a block, soak a tablespoon-size nugget in warm water. Knead the tamarind until it has dissolved and the water is a deep brown color. This is tamarind water or tamarind liquid. Avoid buying tamarind concentrate as it is too dark and sour and makes your food a very dark color.

RICE VINEGAR

A clear potent vinegar, rice vinegar is used in many Thai dipping sauces. It is best to buy this as it is authentic; however, any plain white wine vinegar could be used instead.

OYSTER SAUCE

This is a condiment originally made from simmering oysters until they were thick and caramelized. The modern version is made by simmering salt, sugar, and corn flour with oyster essence. The result is a highly flavored sauce that is full of umami savory flavorings. It is sweet, salty, and and great with stir-fried greens.

PALM SUGAR

This is made from the cooked sap of the coconut palm. It is sold in blocks, nuggets, or compressed cakes. Palm sugar can vary in color and texture, some are more like fudge and others are dark and very hard. The best is a golden brown and has a nutty toffee aroma and taste. If it's not available, you can use golden brown sugar, but it will not be quite the same.

TAMARIND PASTE

SHRIMP PASTE

PALM SUGAR

SOY SAUCE

15
MUST-HAVE
HERBS &
SPICES

·1·
LEMONGRASS

*Spiced shrimp cakes on
lemongrass sticks, p. 30*

Grilled shrimp & basil salad, p. 62

*Isaan-style grilled chicken with
black pepper & lemongrass, p. 84*

*Roasted duck soup with lime,
chile & basil, p. 170*

*Sesame-seared tuna with
lemongrass & ginger, p. 124*

·2·
GINGER

*Braised mushrooms with ginger
& chile, p. 192*

*Grilled fish with garlic,
chile & ginger, p. 148*

*Tea-smoked trout with toasted
coconut & ginger, p. 140*

*Hot & sour soup with roasted shallots,
chicken & Thai basil, p. 168*

*Thai beef skewers with
red chile vinegar, p. 88*

·3·
BLACK & WHITE
PEPPERCORNS

*Sesame chicken salad with
white pepper, p. 64*

*Siamese chicken with ginger, cilantro,
garlic & white pepper, p.98*

*Stir-fried spinach with garlic
& black pepper, p. 194*

*Watermelon with lime, salt
& black pepper, p. 210*

Red curry paste, p. 223

·4·
FIVE SPICE

*Thai beef skewers with
red chile vinegar, p. 88*

*Crispy chicken spring rolls with
chile & ginger, p. 28*

Pork & pickled cucumber salad, p. 72

*Stir-fried cod with sugar snap peas,
ginger & five spice, p. 134*

·5·
THAI BASIL

Grilled shrimp & basil salad, p. 62

*Stir-fried mussels & clams with
chile jam, p. 146*

*Hot & sour soup with roasted shallots,
chicken & Thai basil, p. 168*

Red curry with chicken, p. 156

*Roasted duck soup with lime,
chile & basil, p. 170*

·6·
CORIANDER SEEDS

*Salt & spice roasted pork belly,
p. 100*

*Siamese chicken with ginger, cilantro,
garlic & white pepper, p. 98*

Aromatic smoked fish, p. 138

Salt & pepper mix, p. 246

*Geng Gari spiced curry with
roasted chicken, p. 166*

·7·
CHILE

Chile tamarind caramel, p. 235

Hot & sour green mango salad, p. 60

Thai green curry with shrimp, p. 154

Chicken & coconut milk soup, p. 172

Glass noodle & pork spring rolls, p. 24

*Crab & lime salad with cilantro
& chile, p. 74*

·8·
CILANTRO ROOTS

Fried crab cakes with cilantro, p. 50

*Thai beef skewers with
red chile vinegar, p. 88*

Creamy pumpkin soup, p. 158

*Braised chicken with rice, turmeric
& spices, p. 186*

Hot & sour orange curry paste, p. 227

·9·
STAR ANISE

Salt & spice roasted pork belly, p. 100

Aromatic smoked fish salad, p. 70

*Pineapple with caramelized
chile caramel, p. 208*

Sweet & crispy pork spare ribs, p. 110

*Roasted fruits with Thai
aromatic spices, p. 218*

·10·
CARDAMOM

Spiced banana fritters, p. 200

*Fragrant chicken wings
with galangal, p. 90*

Salt & spice roasted pork belly, p. 100

*Spiced marinade for duck
& chicken, p. 230*

Coconut cream pudding, p. 158

·11·
LIME LEAVES

*Thai fish cakes with
cucumber pickle, p. 48*

*Cured shrimp with ginger
& lime leaves, p. 36*

Coconut fish curry, p. 152

*Spicy beef noodles with
sliced lime leaves, p. 180*

Chicken & coconut milk soup, p. 172

·12·
GARLIC

*Fried crab cakes with
cilantro, p. 50*

Tamarind fried beef with peanuts, p. 86

Green chile nam jim, p. 237

Sweet chile sauce, p. 238

Marinated shrimp satay, p. 144

*Grilled squid with garlic &
black pepper, p. 40*

·13·
TURMERIC

*Chicken satay with turmeric
& ginger, p. 32*

Turmeric grilled fish, p. 130

Grilled pork & herb salad, p. 92

Coconut fish curry, p. 152

Southern Thai grilled chicken, p. 44

*Caramelized chile roasted chicken,
p. 112*

·14·
CINNAMON

Banana & coconut pancakes, p. 214

*Fragrant chicken wings with
galagal, p. 90*

Hot & sour grilled beef salad, p. 56

Aromatic smoked fish, p. 138

*Toasted coconut ice cream topping,
p. 212*

·15·
CUMIN SEEDS

Salt & pepper mix, p. 138

*Mussaman curry paste with
toasted peanuts, p. 228*

*Siamese chicken with ginger, cilantro,
garlic & white pepper, p. 98*

*Geng gari curry with
roasted chicken, p. 166*

Snacks

& Finger Food

chapter 1

Glass Noodle & Pork Spring Rolls

Street food is enjoyed by everyone across Thailand. There are hundreds of variations of spring rolls using different filling ingredients. This is one of my favorites.

serves 6
••••••
(3 per person)

preparation
10 minutes

soaking
10 minutes

cooking
5 minutes per batch

fresh

1 lb lean ground pork

2 garlic cloves, finely chopped

2 red chiles, seeded and finely chopped

3 cilantro sprigs, leaves picked and roughly chopped

Green Chile Nam Jim Sauce (see page 237), to serve

spices

1 tablespoon freshly ground black pepper

pantry

½ lb thin glass noodles or rice noodles

1 tablespoon fish sauce

½ teaspoon salt

1 teaspoon golden brown sugar

1 cup vegetable oil

spring roll wrappers (3 per person)

1. Soak the noodles in a bowl of cold water for 10 minutes to soften. Drain, then put the noodles in a saucepan of lightly salted boiling water and cook until al dente, about 4 minutes. Strain, then run under cold water to refresh them. Use a pair of scissors to cut the noodles into ¾-inch lengths.

2. Put the minced pork in a large bowl and add the chopped noodles, fish sauce, salt, sugar, and black pepper. Mix together, then add the garlic, chiles, and cilantro and mix again.

3. Heat a small amount of oil in a frying pan over medium heat, and once hot enough, fry a small ball of meat mixture for a few minutes until cooked. Taste the meat to check the balance of flavors and adjust if needed, remembering that the dipping sauce will be salty, hot, and sour, too.

4. Use the spring roll wrappers and prepared filling to roll the springs rolls following the instructions on pages 26–27.

5. Prepare the oil as instructed on page 27 and fry the spring rolls in small batches for about 4 minutes, moving the spring rolls around in the pan and turning them so they become golden brown all over.

6. Using a slotted spoon, transfer the rolls to a paper towel–lined plate to drain any excess oil. Allow the oil to reheat for a minute before cooking the next batch. Serve with Green Chile Nam Jim Sauce for dipping.

how to make

SPRING ROLLS

makes: 18 * preparation: 10 minutes * cooking: 5 minutes per batch

equipment: small bowl of water, pastry brush, clean kitchen
towel, lightly oiled platter or plate, wok, vegetable oil for deep-frying

1 LAY

*a spring roll wrapper on a clean kitchen towel. Repeat
with two others – you can work on three at a time.
Place 1 tablespoon of filling on the wrapper about
1¼ inch from the edge nearest to you.*

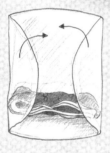

2 FOLD

in the left and right sides.

3 GENTLY FOLD

*the bottom edge up over the filling and roll it tightly away
from you like a cigar. It is important to roll it tightly so that
it is not baggy.*

4 DAB

a little water on the edge of the wrapper using a pastry brush.

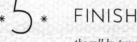

5 FINISH

*the roll by pressing the edges against each other to seal like
a package. Repeat with the other two wrappers and place
on a lightly oiled plate.*

There are hundreds of variations for the fillings and dipping sauces for Thai spring rolls. You can easily use some leftovers to make a delicious snack – a few shrimp or some cooked chicken or pork will go a long way when mixed with some herbs and other aromatic ingredients to make the filling.

* 6 *

PLACE

a wok or a high-sided heavy-bottomed pan over medium-high heat. Heat for a couple of minutes before filling the wok one-third full with vegetable oil ready for deep-frying (the oil can be reused when cool). To test if the oil is hot enough for frying, drop a small piece of bread into the oil. It should sizzle and give off bubbles right away. If it doesn't, remove the bread and try again. When the oil is hot enough, reduce the heat slightly to keep a constant temperature.

FRY

the spring rolls in small batches so that the oil remains hot. Using a slotted spoon, move the spring rolls around the wok for about 4 minutes, turning them so they become golden brown all over. Using a slotted spoon, transfer the cooked spring rolls to a paper towel–lined plate to drain any excess oil. Allow the oil to reheat for a minute before cooking the next batch. Serve with dipping sauce and fresh herbs.

* 7 *

Good spring rolls are delicate in size and shape – 1¼ inch wide and 2½–3 inches long. Make sure that they are tight and firm when rolling and don't make them too big.

CHEF'S TIP

Put the dipping sauce and the serving herbs in bowls in the center of the table. Take a hot spring roll, wrap a couple of herb leaves around it, dip into the sauce, and enjoy.

Crispy Chicken Spring Rolls
with chile & ginger

serves 4
● ● ● ●
(3 per person)

preparation
50 minutes

cooking
15 minutes
per batch

fresh

2 garlic cloves, finely chopped

1 red chile, finely chopped

1½-inch piece of ginger, peeled and grated

½ lb oyster mushrooms, finely chopped

2 oz onion, finely chopped

½ lb ground chicken

4 spring onions, finely chopped

2 eggs

a handful of cilantro, leaves picked and roughly chopped (reserve some whole leaves for a garnish)

Sweet Chile Sauce (see page 238) or Hot and Sour Chile Sauce (see page 234), to serve

spices

1 teaspoon five-spice powder

freshly ground black pepper

pantry

1 cup vegetable oil

¼ teaspoon salt

2 tablespoons fish sauce

spring roll wrappers to make spring rolls (3 per person)

Simply wrap the fried spring rolls in a couple of lettuce leaves and dip in the sauce to enjoy.

1. Heat a heavy-bottomed pan over high heat. Add a little oil, then add the garlic, chile, and ginger. Turn the heat down to medium and fry until fragrant and aromatic, about 2 minutes. Add the mushrooms and the onion, turn up the heat and fry quickly until they are browned with a nutty aroma. Season with the salt and black pepper.

2. Mix the chicken, spring onions, eggs, cilantro, five-spice powder and fish sauce in a large bowl and add the fried mixture. Heat a tiny bit of oil in a frying pan over medium heat and fry a small piece of the mixture for a minute or two until cooked. Taste it and adjust the seasoning if needed, remembering that the dipping sauce will be hot, salty and sour.

3. Use the spring roll wrappers and prepared filling to roll the springs rolls following the instructions on pages 26–27.

4. Prepare the oil as instructed on page 27 and fry the spring rolls in small batches for about 5 minutes, moving the spring rolls around in the pan and turning them so they become golden brown all over. Using a slotted spoon, remove the rolls and transfer to a paper towel–lined plate to drain any excess oil. Allow the oil to reheat for a minute before cooking the next batch. To eat, wrap a few cilantro leaves around the spring rolls, before dipping in your chosen dipping sauce.

Chao Tom

spiced shrimp cakes on lemongrass sticks

serves 6
• • • • •
(makes 24)

preparation
10 minutes

cooking
4 minutes

Chao Tom is a spiced shrimp paté, which can be grilled, fried, or wrapped in banana leaves and steamed. The lemongrass sticks infuse the shrimp paté with a lovely aromatic flavor.

fresh

12 lemongrass stalks

2 lb large raw tiger shrimp, peeled and deveined

1 egg white

2 garlic cloves, finely chopped

1¼-inch piece of ginger, peeled and finely chopped

2 red chiles, seeded and finely chopped

a handful of cilantro, leaves picked and roughly chopped

juice of 1 lime

Green Chile Nam Jim (see page 237), to serve

spices

freshly ground black pepper

pantry

1 tablespoon fish sauce

1 tablespoon rice flour

salt

1. Trim the root end of the lemongrass, but leave the core which will hold the stem together. Cut the stems to about 4–5 inches in length. Remove the tough outer leaves and cut the stems in half through the core so that you have 24 sticks held in place by the core.

2. Place all the ingredients, except the lemongrass, in a food processor or blender, add some salt and black pepper and blend into a paste. Do not over-blend or the mixture will become tough. Fry a small piece of the mixture so that you can taste and adjust the seasoning accordingly.

3. Preheat a grill or grill pan over high heat. Roll the mixture into balls and press a lemongrass stick into each one. Mold the paté around the stem like a lollipop. Grill the shrimp cakes on the hot grill or grill pan for about 2 minutes on each side until golden brown on both sides and the meat is firm. Serve with a dipping sauce, such as Green Chile Nam Jim Sauce.

CHEF'S TIP This recipe is traditionally made using sugar cane sticks, but as they are quite hard to find I have used lemongrass here, which imparts its unique perfume right into the center of the fishcakes.

Chicken Satay
with turmeric & ginger

serves 4-6
• • • • • • • • •

preparation
10 minutes

marinating
1 hour

cooking
18 minutes

Satay essentially means "stick," and there are scores of different satay recipes in Thailand. These ones are great with the flavors of lemongrass and turmeric.

fresh

2 onions, chopped

2-inch piece of ginger, peeled and grated

2 lemongrass stalks, finely chopped

2 garlic cloves, finely chopped

2 medium-hot red chiles, seeded and finely chopped

juice of 1 lime

2 lb chicken thighs, cut into 1¼-inch cubes

Peanut Dipping Sauce (see page 242), to serve

spices

½ teaspoon freshly ground black pepper

2 teaspoons ground turmeric

pantry

2 tablespoons fish sauce

1 tablespoon tamarind paste

½ teaspoon salt

bamboo skewers soaked in cold water for 30 minutes

1. Put the onions, ginger, lemongrass, garlic, and chiles in a food processor or blender and blend until smooth. Add the lime juice, fish sauce, tamarind paste, salt, and black pepper and blend again.

2. Pour the blended ingredients into a heavy-bottomed pan, add the turmeric, and stir well. Simmer gently over medium-high heat until the onions are cooked, about 10 minutes. Let cool.

3. Place the chicken in a shallow dish, pour the fried mixture over the chicken, and thoroughly mix together so that the chicken is completely coated. Cover the dish with plastic wrap and marinate the chicken in the refrigerator for at least 1 hour.

4. Thread the chicken onto the soaked skewers, allowing 3 pieces of chicken per skewer.

5. Preheat the broiler or grill to high heat and broil the chicken until cooked through and browned, about 4 minutes on each side. To check that it is cooked, cut open one piece – the meat should be white inside, not pink. Serve with Peanut Dipping Sauce.

Tod Man Khao Phad
curried sweet corn fritters

serves 4-6

• • • • • • • • •

preparation
10 minutes

cooking
4–6 minutes
per batch

These crispy fritters are great when made with really sweet and crunchy fresh corn kernels. The curry paste added to the batter makes them a perfect snack because the flavors stimulate all the taste buds.

fresh

4 ears corn

2 tablespoons Red or Green Curry Paste (see pages 223 and 224)

2 large eggs

4 spring onions, finely chopped

a handful of cilantro, leaves picked and roughly chopped

spices

freshly ground black pepper

pantry

6 tablespoons rice flour

1 tablespoon fish sauce

1 tablespoon light soy sauce

¼ teaspoon salt

vegetable oil, for frying

to serve

lime wedges and/or a dipping sauce made from lime juice or rice vinegar

1. Use a sharp knife to slice the kernels from the corn, but don't cut too much of the lower end of the husk, nearest the core of the cob.

2. In a large bowl, mix together the flour, curry paste, eggs, fish sauce, soy sauce, salt, and pepper. Add the corn kernels, spring onions, and cilantro and mix well. If the batter is a little dry, stir in 2 tablespoons water.

3. Heat enough oil for frying the fritters in a large heavy-bottomed pan over medium-high heat. When the oil is hot enough (see step 6 on page 27 for how to test if the oil is hot enough). Drop a tablespoon of the batter into the oil and use the back of the spoon to flatten the mixture into a rough patty or cake. Add a few more tablespoons of batter to the oil and cook until golden brown and fragrant, 2–3 minutes on each side. Cook only a few at a time so that the oil does not drop in temperature.

4. Using a slotted spoon, transfer the cooked fritters to a paper towel–lined plate to drain any excess oil. Serve hot or at room temperature with lime wedges or a sour dipping sauce made with lime juice or rice vinegar.

Kung Sang Wa
cured shrimp with ginger & lime leaves

serves 4
●●●●

preparation
10 minutes

cooking
4 minutes

This refreshing salad is quick to make and perfect for a party appetizer.

fresh

12 large raw shrimp, shell on

2 tablespoons lime juice

2 tablespoons orange juice

5 lime leaves, finely sliced

2 lemongrass stalks, tough outer leaves removed and stalks sliced

3 spring onions, finely chopped

1½-inch piece of ginger, peeled and grated

2 medium-hot red chiles, seeded and finely chopped

4 mint sprigs, leaves picked

4 cilantro sprigs, leaves picked

pantry

2 tablespoons fish sauce

½ teaspoon superfine sugar

1. Preheat a grill or grill pan to high heat. Grill the shrimp for 2 minutes on each side. Once cooked, peel and devein the shrimp, then finely shred the meat and set aside.

2. In a large bowl, mix the lime and orange juices with the fish sauce and sugar and stir to dissolve. Add the shrimp and sliced lime leaves and leave to cure for 3 minutes.

3. Add the remaining ingredients to the shrimp, adding the herbs last, and stir gently to mix. Taste to check the balance of flavors and adjust the seasoning to suit your taste.

CHEF'S TIP

You can use other grilled shellfish here, such as crayfish, lobster, or crab, which also provide the sweet richness needed in this dish.

Tamarind Fried Shrimp

The shrimp are sweet and juicy, the tamarind is sour, the soy sauce is caramelized and salty, and the chile and black pepper are hot. You could also use this marinade for fish, other shellfish, chicken, or pork. Serve them as a starter with some cucumber slices or as part of a large meal with salads and roasted meats.

serves 4-6

• • • • • • • • •

preparation
5 minutes

marinating
30 minutes

cooking
4 minutes

fresh
1 lb raw shrimp, peeled and
deveined

spices
1 teaspoon freshly ground black
pepper
¼ teaspoon red pepper flakes

pantry
2 tablespoons tamarind paste
1 tablespoon light soy sauce
½ teaspoon soft brown sugar
pinch of salt
2 tablespoons vegetable oil,
for cooking

1. In a large bowl, mix together the black pepper, pepper flakes, tamarind paste, soy sauce, and brown sugar. Add the shrimp, cover, and refrigerate for 30 minutes, turning the shrimp 2–3 times during the marinating time.

2. Remove the bowl from the refrigerator and season the shrimp with salt. Heat the cooking oil in pan over medium-high heat and fry the shrimp until they are dark brown, about 2 minutes on each side. Serve right away.

CHEF'S TIP

If you add the salt to the marinade, the shrimp would leach out their liquid and juice, causing them to dry out and taste too salty.

serves 4
• • • •

preparation
10 minutes

cooking
3 minutes

Grilled Squid
with garlic & pepper

Dishes like this are found all around the coast of Thailand and Southeast Asia. There are as many variations as there are little hawker stalls and portable grills selling them on the streets.

fresh

2 garlic cloves, finely chopped

3 small green chiles, seeded and finely chopped

1½-inch piece of ginger, peeled and grated

juice of 1 lemon

3 large squid (bodies about 6–9 inches long), cleaned, body and tentacles removed, and scored (see page 116 or ask your fishmonger to do this)

spices

½ teaspoon ground white pepper

pantry

2 tablespoons fish sauce

1 teaspoon grated palm sugar (or coconut sugar or soft brown sugar)

salt

vegetable oil, for brushing

1. Preheat the grill or broiler to high heat.

2. For the dipping sauce, mix the garlic, chiles, ginger, lemon juice, and fish sauce together in a bowl. Stir in the palm sugar.

3. Pat the squid dry with paper towels and season with salt and the white pepper.

4. Brush the hot grill or broiler with a little oil. Grill the squid on the unscored side first for 90 seconds. Using tongs, turn the squid over and cook on the scored side for 60 seconds. Serve the grilled squid with the green chile and garlic dipping sauce.

Miang of Shrimp

serves 4
••••

preparation
10 minutes

cooking
7 minutes

This little dish has all the characteristics of authentic Thai cuisine. It is absolutely delicious and quite complex, which is why it works well as a small bite-size taste explosion.

fresh

¾-inch piece of ginger, grated, plus a 1¼-inch piece of ginger, finely diced

4 tablespoons toasted coconut

2 red chiles, seeded and finely chopped

1 lime, ½ juiced and the rest peeled and cut into small dice

½ lb cooked shrimp, peeled, deveined, and chopped if large

4 small shallots, finely diced

2 tablespoons blanched peanuts, toasted until golden brown and coarsely ground using a mortar and pestle

1 lemongrass stalk, tough outer leaves removed and finely diced

8 Little Gem lettuce leaves, for serving

pantry

1 teaspoon shrimp paste (see page 18)

2 tablespoons fish sauce

1 tablespoon palm sugar

1. Heat a frying pan over high heat. Once hot, add the grated ginger and shrimp paste to the pan. Fry, stirring, until the mixture is aromatic and golden, about 3 minutes.

2. Transfer the cooked mixture to a mortar and add half the toasted coconut and the chiles. Grind with a pestle until smooth.

3. Return the mixture to the pan and add the fish sauce, palm sugar, and 6 tablespoons water. Simmer until the sauce is reduced by half, about 7 minutes, then add the lime juice. Taste to check the balance of flavors – the sauce should be sweet, sour, and salty with the heat coming from the fresh chile.

4. Mix the shrimp with the diced lime, diced ginger, 4 tablespoons of the sauce, the remaining coconut, the shallots, peanuts, and lemongrass in a large bowl. To serve, spoon the mixture onto the Little Gem lettuce leaves.

Southern Thai Grilled Chicken

There is a flavorful balance of hot, sweet, salt, and sour in these little chicken strips. They are deliciously spicy and will have your friends lining up for more.

serves 4
••••

preparation
5 minutes

cooking
10 minutes

fresh

2 garlic cloves, finely chopped

1 small onion, chopped

¾ lb skinless chicken breast, cut into ¼-inch slices

juice of 1 lime

4 cilantro sprigs, leaves picked, for garnish

spices

1 teaspoon medium-hot curry powder

1 teaspoon ground coriander

½ teaspoon ground ginger

½ teaspoon ground turmeric

pantry

2 tablespoons vegetable oil

¼ cup coconut cream

2 tablespoons fish sauce

1 teaspoon honey

1. Heat the vegetable oil in a wok or frying pan over medium-high heat and sauté the garlic until golden brown, being careful not to let it burn. Add the onion, reduce the heat and stir-fry quickly until the onion is softened, about 3 minutes.

2. Add the curry powder, ground coriander, ginger, and turmeric and cook for 1 minute until the spices are fragrant and aromatic. Add the coconut cream, fish sauce, and honey and simmer for 2 minutes. Remove from the heat and let cool.

3. Preheat a grill or grill pan to hot.

4. When the curry paste has cooled, mix in the slices of chicken and stir to coat.

5. Grill the chicken on the hot grill or grill pan for 3 minutes on each side. Turn the chicken regularly so that it does not stick.

6. Remove the chicken from the grill, squeeze over the lime juice and garnish with cilantro leaves torn over the top.

how to make
THAI FISH CAKES

makes: 24 * preparation: 10 minutes * cooking: 10 minutes

With this classic street-food dish it is important that the fish cakes are tender but not too soft. You can vary the types of fish and flavorings – use more herbs, add curry paste to increase the heat, or use a combination of fish and crabmeat or fish and prawn.

 equipment: food processor, mortar and pestle, lightly oiled tray or plate, wok, vegetable oil for deep-frying

1

GRIND

1 lb white fish fillets in a food processor or blender for a few seconds – a little texture is good, so fish doesn't have to be finely ground.

GRIND

2 garlic cloves, 2 cleaned and chopped cilantro roots, 1 finely sliced shallot, 3 seeded and finely chopped red chiles, and a 1½-inch piece of peeled and roughly chopped ginger with ½ teaspoon salt using a mortar and pestle until you have a smooth paste.

2

3 TRANSFER

to a bowl with the ground fish and add 1 tablespoon fish sauce. Mix everything together thoroughly, kneading the mixture with your fingers and really squeezing it together.

4 PICK

up a small handful of the mixture and throw it firmly against the side of the bowl with a slap and a flick of the wrist. Repeat the process constantly for 3–4 minutes. This may seem like an odd step, but it makes the fish more tender because you are breaking down the proteins to tenderize the fish.

5 LIGHTLY

oil your hands and roll the mixture into 20 balls. When you are ready to cook them, pat the balls into flat cakes about 2 inches wide and ³/₈ inch thick.

6 HEAT

the oil to 400°F in a wok or deep-sided heavy-bottomed pan. Fry the fish cakes in small batches until golden brown, about 2–3 minutes. Drain on paper towels and serve with a dipping sauce.

CHEF'S TIP

If you want to prepare them in advance, you can keep the shaped fish cakes on a plate or an oiled baking sheet in the refrigerator before cooking them.

serves 6
•• •• ••
(makes 24)

preparation
10 minutes

chilling
30 minutes

cooking
10 minutes

fresh

1 lb white fish fillets such as cod, coley, or ling

2 garlic cloves

2 cilantro roots, cleaned and chopped

4 shallots, finely sliced

4 long red chiles, halved, seeded and finely chopped

1½-inch piece of ginger, peeled and grated

¼ lb green beans, finely sliced

5 lime leaves, finely chopped

1 cucumber, finely sliced

juice of 1 lime

4 cilantro sprigs, leaves picked and roughly chopped

pantry

1 teaspoon salt

1 tablespoon fish sauce

⅓ cup rice vinegar

2 tablespoons superfine sugar

2 tablespoons toasted crushed peanuts

vegetable oil, for deep-frying

Thai Fish Cakes
with cucumber pickle

This is a great street-food dish and perfect to greet your guests with along with a drink at the beginning of a meal.

1. Put the fish in a food processor or blender and whirl for a few seconds. A little texture is good—the fish doesn't have to be blended until completely fine.

2. Using a mortar and pestle, grind the garlic, cilantro roots, 1 of the shallots, 3 of the red chiles, the ginger, and ½ teaspoon salt until you have a smooth paste. Transfer to a large bowl along with the ground fish, fish sauce, and beans. Knead the mixture with your fingers until thoroughly mixed together.

3. Tenderize the mixture by following step 4 on page 47.

4. Lightly oil your hands. Roll the mixture into 24 small balls and place them on an oiled baking sheet or platter. Refrigerate the balls for 30 minutes.

5. While the fish cakes are chilling, make the cucumber pickle. Warm the vinegar, sugar, and the remaining ½ teaspoon salt together in a nonreactive saucepan to dissolve the sugar. Simmer for 1 minute, then leave to cool. When the vinegar is cool, add the cucumber, the remaining shallots, and the chiles and stir gently. Add the lime juice, chopped cilantro, and toasted peanuts. Set aside.

6. When ready to fry the cakes, pat them into flat cakes about 2 inches wide and ⅜ inch thick. Fry the fish cakes following the instructions on page 47. Drain the fish cakes on a paper towel–lined plate. Serve with the cucumber pickle.

Fried Crab Cakes
with cilantro

Crabmeat is deliciously sweet and provides a lovely texture to these crab cakes.

serves 6
●●●●●●
(makes 30)

preparation
10 minutes

chilling
30 minutes

cooking
10 minutes

fresh

¾ lb white fish fillets, such as cod, coley, or ling

2 garlic cloves, chopped

2 cilantro roots, cleaned and chopped

3 long green chiles, halved, seeded and finely chopped

1½-inch piece of ginger, peeled and grated

3 spring onions, finely chopped

3 cilantro sprigs, leaves picked and roughly chopped

3 basil sprigs, leaves picked and roughly chopped

¾ lb cooked crabmeat, picked over

Sweet Chile Sauce
(see page 238), to serve

pantry

½ teaspoon salt

1 tablespoon fish sauce

vegetable oil, for deep-frying

1. Place the fish in a food processor or blender and whirl for a few seconds. A little texture is good—the fish doesn't have to be blended until completely fine.

2. Using a mortar and pestle, grind the garlic, cilantro roots, green chiles, ginger, and salt until you have a smooth paste. Transfer to a large bowl along with the minced fish, fish sauce, and spring onions. Thoroughly mix everything together.

3. Tenderize the mixture by following step 4 on page 47. When finished, add the cilantro, basil, and crabmeat and mix together.

4. Lightly oil your hands. Roll the mixture into 30 small balls and place them on an oiled baking sheet or platter. Refrigerate the balls for 30 minutes.

5. Fry the crab cakes following the instructions in step 6 on page 47. Drain the crab cakes on paper towels and serve with the Sweet Chile Sauce.

Salads

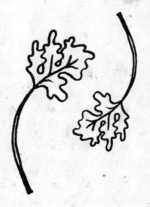

chapter 2

serves 4

• • • •

preparation
10 minutes

Shrimp Noodle Salad
with chile & toasted cashew nuts

This dish is a visual feast of contrasting colors
and textures that look vibrant and exciting
on the plate.

fresh

1 red chile, seeded and finely
chopped

1½-inch piece of ginger, peeled
and grated

juice of 2 limes

½ lb cooked thin rice noodles,
drained and chilled

½ lb cooked shrimp, peeled and
halved

4 spring onions, finely chopped

4 mint sprigs, leaves picked and
torn

4 cilantro sprigs, leaves picked

spices

freshly ground black pepper

pantry

2 tablespoons light soy sauce

1 tablespoon blended sesame oil

3 tablespoons toasted cashew
nuts

salt

1. In a large bowl, mix the chile, ginger, and lime juice together.
Add the soy sauce and sesame oil, and stir together. Add the noodles
and shrimp and mix together. Add the spring onions and season well
with a little salt and lots of black pepper.

2. When ready to serve, add the mint and cilantro leaves to the
noodles and mix together. (Only add the mint and cilantro when
you are ready to serve the salad, because the acidity of the dressing
will turn the leaves black.) Scatter over the toasted cashew nuts. Taste
the noodles to check the balance of flavors and adjust the seasoning
if needed.

Hot & Sour
Grilled Beef Salad
with toasted rice & cilantro

serves 4
• • • •

preparation
10 minutes

cooking
6–8 minutes

All the elements in this dish are present – hot, sweet, salt, and sour. The beef is sweet and rich and the dressing is a perfect accompaniment.

fresh

1 lb top round steak

2 long red chiles, seeded and finely chopped

3 spring onions, finely sliced

½ bunch of cilantro, leaves picked

12 mint leaves, half of them finely sliced

juice of 3 limes

spices

freshly ground black pepper

1 teaspoon ground cinnamon

1 teaspoon ground cumin

1 teaspoon ground coriander

pantry

salt

2 tablespoons light soy sauce

4 tablespoons ground toasted rice (see page 17) or toasted sesame seeds

1. Season the beef with salt, pepper, cinnamon, cumin, coriander, and pepper, making sure that the meat is evenly coated.

2. Preheat a grill, grill pan, or broiler until hot. Grill the beef for 6–8 minutes for medium-rare (or longer or shorter if preferred). Remove from the heat and let rest for 5 minutes, reserving the roasting juices. Slice the beef.

3. In a serving bowl, stir together the chiles, spring onions, cilantro, mint, and lime juice. Add the beef and the reserved juices and toss, then add the soy sauce and toss again.

4. Add half the ground rice and mix through. Taste to check the balance of flavors and adjust if needed. Garnish with the remaining ground rice.

CHEF'S TIP

Grilled mushrooms and asparagus make an excellent vegetarian alternative to the beef.

Asian Noodle Salad
with roasted duck & sesame seeds

serves 6
●●●●●●
(makes 24)

soaking
10 minutes

preparation
10 minutes

cooking
5 minutes

Roasted duck is sweet and rich, but the flavor of lime in this salad will cut through the richness to make a really luscious, fresh-tasting salad.

fresh

1½-inch piece of ginger, peeled and grated

1 tablespoon Sweet Chile Sauce (page 238)

juice of 2 limes

1 cucumber, split in half lengthwise, seeded, then cut into diagonal strips

3 spring onions, finely chopped

3 basil sprigs, leaves picked

3 cilantro sprigs, leaves picked

½ a roasted duck, meat shredded

spices

freshly ground black pepper

pantry

¾ lb thin glass noodles (wa sun noodles) or rice noodles

2 tablespoons light soy sauce

1 tablespoon blended sesame oil

salt

2 tablespoons toasted sesame seeds

1. Soak the noodles in a bowl of cold water for 10 minutes to soften. Drain, then put the noodles in a saucepan of lightly salted boiling water and cook for about 4 minutes until al dente. Strain, then run under cold water to refresh them.

2. In a small bowl, mix together the ginger, Sweet Chile Sauce, lime juice, soy sauce, and sesame oil.

3. In another bowl, mix together the noodles, cucumber, and spring onions and add a little salt and lots of black pepper.

4. When ready to serve, tear the basil and cilantro leaves into the noodles and mix together. Sprinkle over the sesame seeds. Taste the noodles to check the balance of flavors and adjust if needed. Drizzle with the sauce and serve the noodle salad with the roasted duck.

Yam Som Tam
hot & sour green mango salad

serves 4-6
•••••••••

preparation
20 minutes

cooking
3–4 minutes

This is a deliciously fresh salad that has variations all over Southeast Asia. You will see vendors grinding the ingredients for this taste sensation at sidewalk stalls, in markets, and on beaches from Hanoi to Singapore.

fresh

2 small bird's-eye chiles, or to taste

2 garlic cloves

2 shallots, finely sliced

6 cherry tomatoes (the less ripe the better), quartered

juice of 2 limes

1 large unripe green papaya or 2 unripe green mangos, peeled, pitted, and flesh cut into matchsticks

a handful of cilantro, leaves picked

pantry

2 tablespoons blanched skinless peanuts

pinch of salt

1¼-inch piece of palm sugar, or 1 teaspoon golden brown sugar

1 tablespoon fish sauce

1. Preheat the oven to 325°F. Spread the peanuts out in a roasting pan or rimmed baking sheet and toast for 3–4 minutes until pale golden.

2. Using a mortar and pestle, grind the chiles, garlic, and salt until you have a smooth paste.

3. Add the shallots, cherry tomatoes, and palm sugar and grind for 1 minute to break up the ingredients and form a rough paste. Keep turning the mixture over from the bottom as you grind so that the paste is completely mixed through.

4. Add the lime juice, fish sauce, and toasted peanuts. Grind until they are broken up so you will get bits of nuts in every mouthful.

5. Put the papaya in a large serving bowl and pour over the dressing. Tear in the cilantro leaves. Taste to check the balance of flavors and adjust if needed.

CHEF'S TIP

You could add some freshly cooked shrimp at the end if you like. This type of salad is a great accompaniment to dishes such as spiced roasted pork or duck curry.

Grilled Shrimp & Basil Salad

serves 4
● ● ● ●

preparation
10 minutes

cooking
4 minutes

Thai basil has an amazing licorice, aniseed taste and often has flowers and stems with a purple shade. It is easy to grow the plant from seeds, but it is widely available from Asian markets and some supermarkets.

fresh

1 lb raw shrimp, peeled

2 long green chiles, seeded and finely chopped

1¼-inch piece of ginger, peeled and grated

1 lemongrass stalk, outer leaves removed, and stalk finely chopped

2 spring onions, finely chopped

grated zest and juice of 1 lime

juice of 1 orange

3 Thai basil sprigs, leaves picked (or use leaves from 2 regular basil sprigs and 1 mint sprig)

spices

freshly ground black pepper

pantry

salt

2 teaspoons grated palm sugar

1 tablespoon fish sauce

1 tablespoon light soy sauce

1. Preheat a grill or grill pan to high heat. Season the shrimp with salt and black pepper. Grill the shrimp for 2 minutes on each side until cooked.

2. Place the chiles, ginger, lemongrass, spring onions, lime zest and juice, and orange juice in a large bowl.

3. Add the palm sugar, fish sauce, soy sauce, and the grilled shrimp and turn them over in the dressing.

4. Let the salad cool in the dressing for a few minutes. When you are ready to serve the salad, tear in the Thai basil, mix together, and serve.

Sesame Chicken Salad
with white pepper

serves 4
● ● ● ●

preparation
10 minutes

poaching
20 minutes

cooking
5 minutes

This vibrant salad comes from northeast Thailand. It has a variety of textures and can be served as a meal in itself accompanied by rice or noodles or could be part of a larger meal.

fresh

4 cilantro sprigs, leaves picked, and stems reserved

6 celery stalks, sliced on the diagonal

1½-inch piece of ginger, peeled and finely chopped (keep the peel)

3 skinless and boneless chicken breasts

2 garlic cloves, finely chopped

2 green chiles, seeded and finely chopped

4 spring onions, finely chopped

spices

6 white peppercorns

1 teaspoon ground white pepper

pantry

2 tablespoons fish sauce

2 tablespoons rice wine vinegar

¼ teaspoon salt

1 teaspoon superfine sugar

2 tablespoons sesame oil

2 tablespoons sesame seeds

1. Bring a pan of water to a boil. Add the cilantro stalks, 2 celery stalks, the ginger peel, and the white peppercorns. When the stock is simmering, add the chicken breasts and return it to a boil. Skim the surface to remove any scum that rises to the surface. Let the chicken simmer for 5 minutes. Cover the pan with a lid and remove from the heat and set aside for 20 minutes – this will result in perfectly cooked, juicy poached chicken. After 20 minutes, use a slotted spoon to remove the chicken from the stock and set aside to cool.

2. Cut the remaining celery stalks into thin slices. In a small saucepan, bring a little water to a boil and parboil the celery for 10 seconds, then refresh it under cold running water to stop the cooking. Drain and set aside.

3. In a small bowl, stir together the garlic, chiles, chopped ginger, spring onions, fish sauce, vinegar, salt, sugar, and white pepper and let stand for the flavors to infuse while you prepare the chicken.

4. Cut the poached chicken into slices that are about ⅜ inch wide and 1¼ inch long. In a serving bowl, mix the chicken with the blanched celery and the sesame oil. Add the dressing and let stand for 5 minutes.

5. In a small frying pan over medium heat, toast the sesame seeds for 3–4 minutes until they pop and turn golden brown, then remove from the heat.

6. Tear the cilantro leaves into the salad and add the toasted sesame seeds. Mix everything together and serve.

Crisp Cabbage & Cilantro Salad

with cashew nuts

serves 4
••••

preparation
15 minutes

With many different shades of green on the plate, this salad is a visual feast. It is often said that we eat with our eyes first, in which case this exciting dish will leave your guests very satisfied.

fresh

1 medium green cabbage, tough outer leaves removed

2 green chiles, seeded and finely chopped

grated zest and juice of 2 limes

1½-inch piece of ginger, peeled and cut into matchsticks

4 spring onions, finely sliced

a bunch of cilantro, leaves picked

½ bunch of mint, leaves picked

pantry

1 tablespoon sesame oil

1 tablespoon light soy sauce

1 tablespoon fish sauce

¾ cup toasted cashew nuts

1. Cut the cabbage into quarters through the core. Using a sharp knife, cut out the core from each quarter and discard. Finely shred the cabbage and place in a large bowl.

2. In a small bowl, mix together the green chiles, lime zest and juice, sesame oil, soy sauce, and fish sauce.

3. In a large bowl, mix together the shredded cabbage, ginger, spring onions, cilantro leaves, and mint leaves. Add two-thirds of the cashew nuts and stir together.

4. When ready to serve, pour the dressing over the salad and toss everything together. Sprinkle over the remaining cashew nuts.

CHEF'S TIP

Dress the salad only when you are ready to serve it, because the dressing is acidic and will cause the herbs to turn black and the crisp nuts to get soggy.

Aromatic Smoked Fish Salad

with Asian herbs & toasted cashew nuts

serves 4-6

● ● ● ● ● ● ● ● ●

preparation
20 minutes

This dish has a striking appearance. Smoking the fish dyes its edges a yellowy orange, which looks fantastic against the vibrant, multicolored salad.

fresh

2 medium-hot red chiles, seeded and finely chopped

juice of 2 limes

2 tablespoons orange juice

3 Aromatic Smoked Fish, filleted (page 138)

1½-inch piece of ginger, peeled and cut into matchsticks

4 spring onions, finely sliced

4 mint sprigs, leaves picked

4 cilantro sprigs, leaves picked

pantry

pinch of salt

2 tablespoons light soy sauce

1 tablespoon rice vinegar

1 teaspoon blended sesame oil

1½ cups toasted cashew nuts

I. Using a mortar and pestle, grind the chiles with a little salt until you have a smooth paste. Add the lime juice, soy sauce, orange juice, vinegar, and sesame oil. Taste the sauce; it should be sour, hot, and salty, and adjust if needed.

2. Flake the smoked fish, removing any bones and the gray flesh that is under the skin.

3. Pour the dressing over the fish and add the nuts, ginger, and spring onions. Tear in the mint and cilantro leaves just before serving.

CHEF'S TIP An oily fish such as mackerel, rainbow trout, or sea mullet is best for this recipe. You could also use a side of salmon. The fish needs to be filleted (ask your fishmonger to do this).

Pork & Pickled Cucumber Salad

The combination of different flavors and textures that give your jaw and taste buds a workout is one of the thrilling things about Southeast Asian food. This dish is no exception.

serves 4-6

● ● ● ● ● ● ● ● ●

preparation
20 minutes

cooking
25 minutes

fresh

1¾ lb pork tenderloin

1 large cucumber, cut in half lengthwise, seeded, and sliced on the diagonal

4 shallots, finely sliced

2 red chiles, seeded and finely chopped

juice of 2 limes

2 cilantro sprigs, leaves picked

3 mint sprigs, leaves picked

spices

1 teaspoon five-spice powder

1 teaspoon ground coriander

freshly ground black pepper

pantry

vegetable oil, for cooking

salt

¾ cup toasted peanuts or cashew nuts

2 tablespoons rice vinegar

1 teaspoon superfine sugar

2 tablespoons fish sauce

1. Preheat the oven to 400°F. Place a little oil in a roasting pan set over medium-high heat. Season the pork with the five-spice powder, ground coriander, pepper, and some salt. Add the pork to the pan and cook for 2 minutes on each side until browned, then transfer the pan to the oven for 20 minutes until cooked. Remove from the oven and let cool.

2. Roughly crush the peanuts using a mortar and pestle. Set aside.

3. Heat the vinegar and sugar in a small pan over medium heat, bring to a simmer, then pour over the cucumber and let cool completely. Add the shallots to the cucumber.

4. Make a dressing by mixing the red chiles with the lime juice and fish sauce. Pour over the cucumber and shallots and toss together.

5. Transfer the pork to a cutting board, and set the roasting pan aside. Pour 2 tablespoons of the dressing into the roasting pan and deglaze the pan, using a wooden spoon to scrape up all the bits and juices left by roasting the pork. Pour this back into the dressing.

6. Slice the pork and add to the cucumber. Tear the cilantro and mint leaves into the dressing (only do this when you are ready to serve). Pour the dressing over the meat and cucumber and mix together. Scatter over the crushed toasted peanuts and serve.

Crab & Lime Salad
with cilantro & chile

serves 4-6
●●●●●●●●●

preparation
10 minutes

This salad is fresh, crisp, and delicious. The crab and cucumber will be sweet or rich and the fresh mint and cilantro provide a refreshing bite to the salad.

fresh

2 long red chiles, seeded and finely chopped

1½-inch piece of ginger, peeled and grated

juice of 2 limes

1 lb white crabmeat, picked over (see Chef's Tip)

1 cucumber, cut in half lengthwise, seeded and cut into diagonal slices

4 spring onions, finely sliced

3 cilantro sprigs, leaves picked

3 mint sprigs, leaves picked

spices

freshly ground black pepper

dressing

1 tablespoon light soy sauce

2 tablespoons fish sauce

1 teaspoon rice vinegar

salt

1. In a small bowl, mix together the chile, ginger, lime juice, soy sauce, fish sauce, and vinegar.

2. In a large bowl, mix together the crabmeat, cucumber, and spring onions. Season well with a little salt and lots of black pepper. Pour the dressing over the crabmeat mixture.

3. When you are ready to serve the salad, tear the cilantro and mint leaves into the salad and mix everything together. (If you add the herbs before you are ready to serve the salad, the acid will cook the leaves and turn them black.) Taste to check the balance of flavors and adjust if needed. Serve right away.

CHEF'S TIP

Try to keep the crabmeat in large pieces so that it is not mashed up, and even when buying picked crabmeat from a fishmonger, always check it again yourself to be sure no shell fragments were missed.

Roasted Duck Salad
with mango & toasted coconut

serves 4
••••

preparation
10 minutes

Roasted duck is delicious with the sweetness and acidity of fresh mango. The tropical picture is completed with the addition of some nutty toasted coconut. What really makes this salad sing and pack a hidden punch is the red chile and raw ginger. The whole dish is awakened by the balance of lime juice and soy sauce. This salad can be a starter or part of a larger meal.

fresh

1 lb roasted duck meat

1 mango, peeled, pitted, and sliced

2 limes – peeled, pith removed, and flesh diced from 1, and just the juice from the other

2 small shallots, finely diced

2 red chiles, seeded and finely chopped

2 tablespoons toasted shredded coconut

3 cilantro sprigs, leaves picked

1¼-inch piece of ginger, peeled and finely grated

8 Little Gem lettuce leaves (optional)

pantry

1 tablespoon grated palm sugar

1 tablespoon light soy sauce

1. Shred the duck meat into small pieces by tearing it with your fingers. In a large bowl, mix the duck with the mango, diced lime, shallots, red chiles, and half the coconut. Tear in the cilantro leaves.

2. To make the dressing, using a mortar and pestle, grind the ginger, palm sugar, and the remaining coconut to a rough paste. Add the soy sauce and lime juice and grind together.

3. Pour the dressing over the duck and toss together. Divide among serving plates, or spoon the mixture into the lettuce leaf cups.

Shrimp Noodle Salad
with mint & toasted peanuts

serves 4
● ● ● ●

preparation
15 minutes

This dish is delicious served cold. You can use any combination of seafood instead of just shrimp, and it is particularly good with crab.

fresh
½ lb cooked large shrimp, chopped

1 red chile, seeded and finely chopped

1¼-inch piece of ginger, peeled and grated

juice of 1 lime

2 spring onions, finely chopped

a handful of bean sprouts

2 cilantro sprigs, leaves picked

spices
freshly ground black pepper

pantry
½ lb thin rice noodles, cooked, drained, and lightly oiled so that they do not stick together

2 teaspoons grated palm sugar

1 tablespoon tamarind paste

1 tablespoon fish sauce

2 tablespoons toasted peanuts

salt

1. In a large bowl, mix the noodles and shrimp together.

2. In a small bowl, make the dressing by mixing the chile, ginger, palm sugar, lime juice, tamarind, and fish sauce together.

3. Pour the dressing over the noodles and shrimp. Add the spring onions and bean sprouts and tear in the cilantro leaves.

4. When you are ready to serve the salad, crush the peanuts using a mortar and pestle and sprinkle over the salad. Season well with salt and black pepper and serve right away.

Roast, Grill & Stir-fry

chapter 3

Kai Yaang Isaan-style Grilled Chicken
with black pepper & lemongrass

serves 4-6

• • • • • • • • •

preparation
15 minutes

marinating
2 hours

cooking
15 minutes

fresh

4 lemongrass stalks, tough
outer leaves removed and
stalks finely sliced

3 cilantro roots, cleaned
and finely chopped

4 garlic cloves

1 long red chile, seeded and
finely chopped

4 chicken thigh fillets, skin on,
cut in half

4 boneless chicken breasts,
skin on and cut into 4 pieces

Red Chile Nam Jim Sauce
(page 236), to serve

spices

2 teaspoons freshly ground
black pepper

pantry

½ teaspoon salt

1 tablespoon fish sauce

2 teaspoons honey

Kai yaang translates as "grilled chicken" and uses a method of rubbing a paste into the meat, marinating, then grilling slowly so that the flavors caramelize on the skin.

1. Using a mortar and pestle, grind the lemongrass with the salt to a rough paste. Add the cilantro roots, garlic, and chile and continue to grind. Add the black pepper and keep mixing and grinding until you have a semi-smooth paste. Add the fish sauce and honey and grind until well blended.

2. In a shallow dish, rub the mixture over the chicken pieces so that they are well coated. Cover the dish with plastic wrap and marinate the chicken in the refrigerator for 2 hours.

3. Preheat a grill pan or charcoal grill. You need the heat to be hot, but you are going to cook the chicken slowly to impart a smoky, savory character and allow the marinade to caramelize on the chicken.

4. If you are using a grill, place the chicken on the hot grill in areas that are not too close to the direct heat. Cook for about 15 minutes, turning the chicken every 3 minutes until the chicken is caramelized on the outside and the meat is cooked. Serve with the Red Chile Nam Sauce.

CHEF'S TIP

Cilantro roots are very important in Thai cooking and are used frequently to make spice rubs and the bases of curry pastes. If the roots are not available, use the lower part of the stems and double the quantity.

serves 4-6
• • • • • • • • •

preparation
10 minutes

marinating
30 minutes

cooking
10 minutes

fresh

2 garlic cloves, finely chopped

2 long red chiles, seeded and finely chopped

1½-inch piece of ginger, peeled and grated

1 lb sirloin, cut into thin slices (or top round; ask your butcher for a cut of meat that you can cook very quickly and is tender)

1 white onion, finely sliced

a small handful of cilantro, leaves picked and roughly chopped

spices

freshly ground black pepper

pantry

2 teaspoons light soy sauce

2 teaspoons fish sauce

2 tablespoons tamarind paste

3 teaspoons granulated sugar

2 tablespoons rice wine vinegar

salt

vegetable oil, for frying

½ cup blanched, skinless peanuts, toasted and roughly chopped, for garnish

Tamarind Fried Beef
with peanuts

This is a simple and very effective beef dish with an extraordinary balance between different textures and the peppery hot, sweet, salt, and sour flavors.

1. Put the garlic, chiles, ginger, soy sauce, fish sauce, and some black pepper in a bowl and mix together. Add the beef and stir to mix, making sure the beef is evenly coated. Cover the bowl with plastic wrap and marinate the beef in the refrigerator for 30 minutes.

2. In a small bowl, dissolve the tamarind paste in 5 tablespoons water, then transfer to a saucepan. Add 2 teaspoons of the sugar and reduce over medium heat to a thick syrup the consistency of honey.

3. Put the onion in a bowl with the vinegar and remaining sugar. Season with salt, mix together, and set aside to semi-pickle for 5 minutes.

4. Heat a little oil in a frying pan over medium heat and fry the marinated beef in batches until golden brown, about 3 minutes, then set aside.

5. Mix the cilantro with the semi-pickled onions and all the juices, then scatter the mixture over a serving platter. Top with the beef, then pour over the caramelized tamarind syrup and garnish with chopped toasted peanuts.

Thai Beef Skewers
with red chile vinegar

The mixture of spice used here is one of the most ancient in Thai cuisine. The blend of hot, sweet, salt, and sour complements the flavor of the beef. It would also work very well with gamey flavors such as quail, pheasant, pigeon, or even venison.

serves 4-6

• • • • • • • • •

preparation
20 minutes

marinating
30 minutes

cooking
10 minutes

fresh

1 lb tender beef, such as round steak, sirloin, or rib eye, trimmed of excess fat and sinew and cut into ¾–1¼-inch cubes

3 cilantro roots, cleaned and chopped

1¼-inch piece of ginger, peeled and sliced

Thai Red Chile Vinegar sauce (page 232), to serve

a handful of cilantro leaves, for garnish (optional)

spices

freshly ground black pepper

20 white peppercorns

½ teaspoon five-spice powder

¼ teaspoon ground turmeric

½ teaspoon ground coriander

pantry

2 tablespoons light soy sauce

pinch of salt

3–4 tablespoons vegetable oil

metal or soaked wooden skewers

1. In a large bowl, mix the soy sauce and a little bit of black pepper and add the beef. Stir to mix, making sure the beef is evenly coated. Cover the bowl with plastic wrap and marinate the beef in the refrigerator for 30 minutes.

2. Crush the cilantro roots, salt, and white peppercorns using a mortar and pestle. Add the ginger, five-spice powder, turmeric, and coriander and continue to grind until well mixed and a coarse paste forms.

3. Add the spice mixture to the meat and stir to coat. Thread the meat onto the skewers, placing 3–4 pieces on each skewer.

4. Heat the oil in grill pan or frying pan over high heat. When hot, add the beef and cook for about 2 minutes on each side until golden brown. Remove the beef from the oil and set aside to rest for a few minutes.

5. Serve with the Thai Red Chile Vinegar sauce and garnish with cilantro leaves. Serve alongside a salad or noodle dish if you like.

CHEF'S TIP

The meat could be also grilled or roasted quickly. Whichever method is used, the meat should be crisp and golden brown on the outside and medium-rare on the inside.

Fragrant Chicken Wings
with galangal

serves 4-6
• • • • • • • • •

preparation
10 minutes

marinating
1 hour

cooking
8–10 minutes

Chicken wings are the perfect quick snack – they are delicious finger food, especially when covered in a spiced marinade. Galangal has a pepper and citrus flavor, and is often peeled, sliced, or grated, then ground into a paste.

fresh

2 garlic cloves, finely chopped

4 cilantro roots, cleaned and finely chopped

2 long green chiles, seeded and finely chopped

1½-inch piece of galangal (or ginger), peeled and grated

1½ lb chicken wings

spices

1 tablespoon coriander seeds, crushed

½ teaspoon ground cinnamon

½ teaspoon red pepper flakes

¼ teaspoon ground cardamom

pantry

2 tablespoons fish sauce

1 tablespoon grated palm sugar

to serve

lime wedges

Sweet Chile Sauce (page 238)

1. In a large bowl, mix together the garlic, cilantro roots, chiles, galangal, the coriander seeds, cinnamon, crushed and pepper flakes, cardamom, fish sauce, and palm sugar.

2. Add the chicken wings and turn to ensure that the wings are well coated in the marinade. Cover the bowl with plastic wrap and marinate the chicken in the refrigerator for 1 hour.

3. Preheat a grill or grill pan to hot. Grill the chicken wings for 8–10 minutes, turning every 2 minutes so that they do not burn. Cut one chicken wing open to check that it is cooked all the way through. Serve with lime wedges and Sweet Chile Sauce.

CHEF'S TIP

Galangal is related to ginger, but has a thicker skin and a more intense aroma and flavor. It needs to be cooked, whereas ginger can be eaten raw. It is available at Asian markets and some supermarkets, either frozen or dried, but if it is not available, use ginger instead.

Grilled Pork & Herb Salad

These spiced and grilled pork chops are rich and flavorful. They pair well with a sour dressing and lots of aromatic fresh herbs.

serves 4
••••

preparation
10 minutes

marinating
1 hour

cooking
8 minutes

fresh

2 garlic cloves, finely chopped

1½-inch piece of ginger, peeled and grated

4 pork chops

3 mint sprigs, leaves picked

3 cilantro sprigs, leaves picked

3 basil sprigs, leaves picked

2 tablespoons bean sprouts, washed

2 spring onions, finely chopped

juice of 2 limes, plus lime wedges to serve

1 tablespoon blended sesame oil

spices

1 tablespoon coriander seeds

1 tablespoon fennel seeds

1 teaspoon ground turmeric

1 teaspoon five-spice powder

½ teaspoon red pepper flakes

freshly ground black pepper

pantry

1 tablespoon vegetable oil

salt

1. Using a mortar and pestle, grind the coriander and fennel seeds together. Add the garlic and ginger and grind to a paste. Pour the paste into a baking dish and add the turmeric, five spice, pepper flakes, some black pepper, and the vegetable oil. Add the pork chops and rub the marinade into the meat so that they are well coated. Cover the dish with plastic wrap and marinate the pork in the refrigerator for at least 1 hour.

2. Preheat the grill or grill pan to hot. When ready to cook, season the pork chops with some salt. Grill the chops for 8 minutes, turning them every 2 minutes so that they do not burn.

3. Meanwhile, make the salad. Tear the herbs into a bowl and add the bean sprouts and spring onions. Dress with the lime juice and sesame oil.

4. When the pork is caramelized and cooked through, set it aside to rest for 5 minutes. Add any juices from the resting meat to the salad, then serve the pork chops with the salad and some lime wedges for squeezing over.

CHEF'S TIP

If you can, choose free-range or organic pork—its flavor will be superior.

Spiced Bavette Steak
with hot & sour sauce

serves 4
• • • •

preparation
5 minutes

marinating
30 minutes

cooking
7–8 minutes

Bavette steak is a delicious cut of beef. It needs to be cooked medium-rare, then left to rest for 5 minutes before slicing. The beef goes well with a crisp cabbage salad with toasted cashew nuts or stir-fried greens with garlic and black pepper.

fresh
1 lb Bavette beef steak
12 mint leaves
½ bunch of cilantro, leaves picked
Hot and Sour Red Chile Sauce (page 234)

spices
1 teaspoon ground coriander
½ teaspoon ground cardamom
½ teaspoon ground nutmeg
½ teaspoon red pepper flakes
1 teaspoon ground ginger
freshly ground black pepper

pantry
salt
1 tablespoon vegetable oil

1. In a large bowl, combine the coriander, cardamom, nutmeg, pepper flakes, ginger, and black pepper. Add the beef and rub the spice mix all over so that it is evenly coated. Cover the bowl with plastic wrap and marinate the beef in the refrigerator for 30 minutes.

2. Preheat a grill, grill pan, or frying pan to hot. When ready to cook, season the meat with a little salt, rub with the oil, and grill the beef for 2 minutes, then turn the meat over and grill for another 2 minutes. Repeat the process and cook the steak to medium-rare, 7–8 minutes total. Remove from the heat and let rest for 5 minutes, reserving all the roasting juices from the grill pan.

3. While the meat is cooking and resting, tear the mint and the cilantro leaves.

4. Slice the rested beef into ⅜-inch-thick slices across the grain and lay on a plate. Mix the herbs with the sauce and the roasting juices and pour over the beef. Taste to check the balance of flavors and add some more sauce if needed.

CHEF'S TIP

Grilled mushrooms and asparagus could be used as a vegetarian alternative here.

Thai Stir-fried Beef

with chile relish

serves 4
• • • •

preparation
15 minutes

cooking
9–11 minutes

Unlike a Chinese stir-fry that would traditionally be served with soy sauce as a condiment, a Thai stir-fry is typically accompanied by the fiery *nam pla* sauce, which is simply chopped hot bird's-eye chiles mixed with fish sauce and a little sugar.

fresh

1 lb tender beef, cut into strips
for stir-frying

3 tablespoons Thai Chile Relish
(page 240)

⅓ lb green beans, trimmed, or
sugar snap peas

4 spring onions, finely sliced

1 large medium-hot red chile,
seeded and finely chopped

a handful of bean sprouts,
washed and trimmed

3 mint sprigs, leaves picked

3 cilantro sprigs, leaves picked

juice of 1 lime

pantry

2 tablespoons vegetable oil

1. Heat a wok over high heat. Add the oil. It will be smoky, so you should begin cooking immediately. Fry one-third of the beef, spreading it out around the pan, until browned, 2–3 minutes, then set aside. Repeat with the remaining beef.

2. Return all the meat to the wok and lower the heat to medium. Add the relish and green beans and cook for 2 minutes.

3. Add the spring onions and cook for 1 minute so that the vegetables are tender but still crisp.

4. Add the chile and bean sprouts and toss together, then add the mint and cilantro leaves and toss together. Add the lime juice and taste; adjust the seasoning to suit your taste.

5. Serve with steamed rice or noodles as a simple meal or as a part of larger selection of dishes.

CHEF'S TIP

When stir-frying, you should have all the ingredients prepped and near the stove before you begin, as the cooking goes quickly. The wok must be on high heat – if the temperature of the wok drops too much, the contents will stew in their own juices, making them soggy rather than fried and golden.

Siamese Chicken
with ginger, cilantro, garlic & white pepper

serves 4-6
• • • • • • • • •

preparation
20 minutes

cooking
10 minutes

Chiles arrived in Thailand after the Spanish and Portuguese journeyed to South America in the sixteenth century. Thai dishes that use white pepper are very old and predate the introduction of chiles to Thai cuisine.

fresh
1 lb chicken thigh fillets, cut into ¾–1¼-inch cubes

3 cilantro roots, cleaned and chopped (if not available, use the lower part of the stems, washed and finely chopped)

1½-inch piece of ginger, peeled and grated

3 garlic cloves

½ a bunch of cilantro, leaves picked

spices
20 white peppercorns

1 tablespoon coriander seeds

½ teaspoon ground turmeric

1 tablespoon cumin seeds

pantry
2 tablespoons light soy sauce

pinch of salt

wooden skewers soaked in cold water for at least 30 minutes

1. In a shallow baking dish, marinate the chicken in the soy sauce while you prepare the rest of the ingredients.

2. Crush the cilantro roots, salt, and peppercorns using a mortar and pestle. Add the ginger, garlic, coriander seeds, turmeric, and cumin seeds and grind until well mixed and a coarse paste forms.

3. Add the spice paste to the chicken and rub the paste all over the cubes to ensure they are well coated. Thread 3 cubes of chicken onto each skewer.

4. Preheat a grill or grill pan to hot. Grill the skewers for 2 minutes on each side, then continue to grill, turning regularly, until cooked, for 3–4 minutes. Alternatively, you can finish cooking the skewers in a preheated 400°F oven for 5 minutes.

5. Garnish with cilantro leaves and serve right away with a green mango salad if you like.

CHEF'S TIP

This dish would also work well with the gamey flavor of quail. Other game birds could be used here too, such as pheasant, pigeon, or squab.

Salt & Spice Roasted Pork Belly

serves 4-6

● ● ● ● ● ● ● ● ●

preparation
10 minutes

cooking
1 hour 25 minutes

This has to be one of the best flavor combinations in the world. If you don't eat pork, then try this combination on a roasted chicken, a butterflied shoulder of lamb, or roasted rib of beef.

fresh
1 pork belly, 3–4 lb total
Peanut Dipping Sauce
(page 242), to serve

spices
3 tablespoons rock salt
1 tablespoon coriander seeds
1 tablespoon cumin seeds
1 tablespoons fennel seeds
10 white peppercorns
1 teaspoon ground cardamom
1 teaspoon five-spice powder
½ teaspoon red pepper flakes

pantry
vegetable oil, for rubbing

1. Preheat the oven to 475°F.

2. Grind the rock salt, coriander seeds, cumin seeds, fennel seeds, and peppercorns using a mortar and pestle until medium-fine in texture. Add the remaining spices, except for the red pepper flakes, and continue to grind until broken up.

3. Put half of the spice mixture in a roasting pan with high-sides and add enough cold water to come ¾ inch up the sides of the pan.

4. Score the pork skin into thin strips. Place the pork belly, skin side down, in the pan with the water – the water should cover the skin and the first deep layer of fat. Place the pan over medium-high heat and bring the water to a boil. Reduce the heat and simmer for about 20 minutes. Simmering the pork in the water dissolves some of the fat and imparts the spicy salt into the pork's skin, making a delicious crackling. After 20 minutes, remove the pork from the water and discard the remaining water. Place a rack in the pan.

5. Place the pork belly, skin side up, on the rack in the pan. Mix the red pepper flakes with the remaining spice mix and rub it into the skin with a little oil.

6. Lower the heat of the oven to 425°F and roast the pork for 20 minutes. Turn the heat down to 350°F and cook for another 40 minutes until the skin is crispy and the meat is soft and cooked.

7. Serve with the Peanut Dipping Sauce and Crisp Cabbage & Cilantro Salad (page 66) if you like.

* 6 ways with *

Chile

 Salt & Chile-Grilled Shrimp

Toast 1 tablespoon coriander seeds, 2 teaspoons fennel seeds, 5 star anise, and 1 cinnamon stick for 2–3 minutes until fragrant.

Grind the spices until medium-fine in a spice grinder or using a mortar and pestle along with ½ teaspoon black peppercorns and a pinch of red pepper flakes.

Season 1 lb raw peeled shrimp with 3 teaspoons of the ground spice mix and a pinch of coarse salt.

Preheat a grill pan or grill to hot. Grill the shrimp for 2 minutes on each side until cooked.

Squeeze the juice of 1 lime over the shrimp and garnish with chopped cilantro leaves.

 Shrimp & Cilantro with Chile & Tamarind

Heat a splash of vegetable oil in a pan and fry 2 seeded and chopped green chiles and 1 tablespoon grated ginger.

Fry until fragrant and aromatic, about 2 minutes.

Add 2 oz tamarind paste and 2 tablespoons light soy sauce.

Remove from the heat and add the juice of 2 limes.

Grill or fry ½ lb large raw peeled shrimp for about 2 minutes on each side.

Dress the shrimp with the chile tamarind dressing and add the leaves from 3 sprigs *each* of cilantro and mint.

 Broiled Pork with Watermelon, Lime & Red Pepper Flakes

Season 1 pork tenderloin and broil under a hot broiler for 12–15 minutes until golden brown and roasted, then let rest for 5 minutes.

Cut half a watermelon into chunks.

Pick the leaves from 3 mint sprigs and tear into the bowl with the watermelon.

Season well with salt. Slice the cooked pork into ¼-inch slices and add to the bowl with the watermelon.

Scatter ¼ teaspoon red pepper flakes over the meat – do not be shy with the salt and the red pepper flakes. Add the juice of 2 limes.

Mix everything together and taste to check the balance of flavors – make sure you can taste hot pepper, sweet watermelon, and some salt and sourness.

 Grilled Green Chile Dip

Grill 4 large whole green chiles, 4 unpeeled garlic cloves, and 4 small unpeeled shallots under a hot grill until the skin is charred and the insides are soft.

Peel the blackened skins from the chiles, garlic, and shallots when they are cool and then grind them all together using a mortar and pestle.

Squeeze in the juice of 1 lime and 1 tablespoon fish sauce and mix into the paste. Taste to check the balance of flavors.

Serve with a side of hard-boiled eggs, slices of cucumber, or beside some grilled meat.

 Crisp Fried Chicken Patties with Green Chile

Dice ½ lb skinless chicken breast into ⅛-inch pieces. Mix 2 teaspoons light soy sauce, 1 teaspoon oyster sauce, and 1 beaten egg together in a bowl and add the chicken.

Crush 2 hot green bird's-eye chiles, 1 garlic clove, and 1 tablespoon grated ginger together using a mortar and pestle. Add to the chicken and mix together.

Mix 3 finely chopped spring onions and the leaves from 3 sprigs each of basil and cilantro together well and add to the chicken mixture. Pick up handfuls of the mixture and slap them firmly back into the bowl. Repeat for 5 minutes to tenderize the meat.

Heat a little vegetable oil in a heavy-bottomed pan. Drop small spoonfuls of the chicken mixture into the hot oil and fry for 3–4 minutes until golden brown and crispy. Cook in small batches so that the oil stays hot.

 Spice-Roasted Squash with Honey & Chile

Cut a butternut squash into 1¼-inch cubes and drizzle 2 tablespoons vegetable oil over the cubes.

Season with a little salt, ½ teaspoon ground coriander, ½ teaspoon ground cumin, ½ teaspoon ground cinnamon, and a pinch of cayenne pepper.

Spread the cubes in a roasting pan and roast in an oven preheated to 400°F for 25 minutes until caramelized.

Heat a splash of vegetable oil in a pan and fry 2 chopped red chiles, 1 tablespoon grated ginger, the grated zest of 1 orange, a pinch of salt, and 2 tablespoons honey until caramelized. Squeeze in the juice of 1 lime.

Pour the fried mixture over the roasted squash and garnish with lime wedges and torn cilantro leaves.

Roasted Pork Shoulder

with coriander, tamarind & chile

serves 6
● ● ● ● ● ●

preparation
10 minutes

cooking
6 hours

resting
15 minutes

fresh
1¼-inch piece of ginger, peeled
and grated
1 pork shoulder, butterflied,
scored, and rolled (ask your
butcher to do this for you),
about 4 lb total
1 red chile, seeded and finely
chopped

spices
1 teaspoon black peppercorns
½ teaspoon cloves
½ teaspoon ground cardamom
1 tablespoon fennel seeds
2 tablespoons coriander seeds
5 star anise
2 cinnamon sticks
½ teaspoon freshly grated
nutmeg
½ teaspoon red pepper flakes

pantry
2 teaspoons salt
3 tablespoons tamarind paste
1 tablespoon sesame oil
1 tablespoon light soy sauce
1 tablespoon honey

The best cut of pork to roast is a shoulder, as
it is layered with meat and fat. The slower and
longer the meat roasts, the slower the fat melts
and keeps the meat really juicy.

1. Preheat the oven to 350°F.

2. Put all the spices, the salt, and the ginger in a spice blender or
clean coffee grinder and blitz until finely ground. Any spices that
you do not use can be stored in an airtight container for another use.

3. Rub the spice blend into the scored skin of the pork shoulder,
being sure to rub it into all the crevices. Place the meat in a
roasting pan and add ¾ cup water to the bottom of the pan.
Roast for 30 minutes to start the pork meat cooking. Reduce the
temperature to 275°F and roast for another 5 hours. Check the
meat regularly and pour all the roasting juices back over the meat.
Do not let the cracklings burn.

4. Remove the meat from the oven and pour the roasting juices
into a pitcher. Spoon off the clear pork fat and keep the darker
roasting juices. Add the tamarind paste, sesame oil, soy sauce, honey,
and chopped red chile to the pitcher and stir together.

5. Raise the oven temperature to 350°F. Pour the tamarind-honey
sauce over the pork and return the pan to the oven for 30 minutes.
Baste the meat with the pan juices 2–3 times to check that crackling
is not burning. Let the meat rest for 15 minutes before carving –
however, it will be more like pulling it apart as the meat will be so
soft. Serve with a crisp salad and Braised Mushrooms (page 192) if
you like.

Wok-fried Chile & Basil Chicken

This is a simple stir-fry that could be eaten on its own or as part of a larger Asian meal where a number of dishes are served in a continuous seamless flow from the kitchen to the table.

serves 4
● ● ● ●
(as part of a
large meal)

preparation
10 minutes

cooking
7–8 minutes

fresh

1½-inch piece of ginger, peeled and grated

2 skinless chicken breasts, cut into the ⅜-inch slices

2 garlic cloves

2 red chiles, seeded and finely chopped

½ lb snow peas

4 spring onions, finely sliced

3 cilantro sprigs, leaves picked

3 basil sprigs, leaves picked

juice of 1 lime

spices

freshly ground black pepper

pantry

2 tablespoons vegetable oil

salt

1 tablespoon light soy sauce

1½ tablespoons fish sauce

1. Heat a wok over medium-high heat. Add half the oil and fry the ginger for 1 minute until fragrant.

2. Add the chicken and stir-fry it briskly, spreading it around the wok so that the slices are in contact with the maximum amount of heat. Fry until golden brown, 3–4 minutes, then season with salt and black pepper.

3. Add the remaining oil and fry the garlic and chiles until fragrant, 1–2 minutes, then add the snow peas.

4. Add the spring onions, soy sauce, and fish sauce and stir-fry for 1 more minute. Stir in the cilantro and basil leaves, together with the lime juice, and serve.

Whole Spice-roasted Poussin
with lemongrass & coconut cream

This dish has an intense depth of flavor that comes from the use of aromatic spices such as lemongrass, ginger, and galangal. Once tried, it will soon become a firm favorite.

serves 4
• • • •

preparation
15 minutes

cooking
40 minutes

fresh

2 small onions, finely diced

2 garlic cloves, crushed

1½-inch piece of ginger, peeled and left whole

¾-inch piece of galangal, peeled and left whole (see Chef's Tip)

4 poussin (young chicken, weighing about 1 lb each; also known as spring chicken)

4 lemongrass stalks, tough outer leaf removed and stems bruised with the back of a heavy knife

juice of 2 limes

pantry

4 dried chiles, soaked in hot water to soften, then water discarded

1 teaspoon salt

1¼ cups coconut cream

2 teaspoons grated palm sugar

1. Preheat the oven to 400°F. Preheat a grill or grill pan to hot.

2. Put the onions, garlic, ginger, and galangal in a food processor and blend to a paste. Add the soaked chiles, salt, and a little water and continue to blend to a smooth paste.

3. Stuff each poussin with the bruised lemongrass and then rub the spice mixture inside and out.

4. Place any remaining spice mixture in a pan with the coconut cream and palm sugar and heat over medium-high heat. Bring to a boil, then simmer until it has reduced by half.

5. Place the poussin on the hot grill and grill for 3–4 minutes on all sides. Transfer the poussin to a roasting pan and roast in the oven for 20 minutes. Baste the poussin with the coconut mixture every 5 minutes until the poussin is tender and the coconut-spice mixture is used up.

6. Pour all the juices from the pan over the poussin and finish with the lime juice. Serve with a rice or noodle dish.

CHEF'S TIP

If galangal is not available, use ginger and double the amount.

Sweet & Crispy Pork Spare Ribs

serves 6
• • • • •

preparation
10 minutes

marinating
2 hours

cooking
6–8 minutes
(per batch)

Pork spare ribs are always a favorite – everyone likes gnawing on delicious bone. This recipe comes from Phuket in the south of Thailand and is very tasty.

fresh

2 garlic cloves, finely chopped

3 cilantro roots, cleaned and finely chopped

1 lb pork spare ribs, cut into short lengths (ask your butcher to do this)

Green Chile Nam Jim Sauce (page 237), to serve

spices

2 teaspoons white peppercorns

2 teaspoons black peppercorns

1 tablespoon coriander seeds

5 star anise

pantry

1 tablespoon golden brown sugar

1 tablespoon dark soy sauce

1 tablespoon fish sauce

1 tablespoon honey

2 tablespoons rice flour

vegetable oil, for deep-frying

1. Using a mortar and pestle, crush the white and black peppercorns, coriander seeds, and star anise until medium fine. Add the garlic, cilantro roots, and brown sugar and grind to a paste. Add the soy sauce, fish sauce, and honey and mix together.

2. Place the ribs in a large bowl and pour the spice mixture over the ribs. Rub the mixture all over the ribs until they are well coated. Cover the bowl with plastic wrap and marinate the ribs in the refrigerator for 2 hours.

3. Place the rice flour in a shallow dish. Remove the ribs from the marinade, dip them in the flour to coat, and shake off any excess.

4. Heat the oil in a wok until it registers 400°F on a deep-frying thermometer or until a cube of bread dropped in browns in 15 seconds. Deep-fry the ribs in small batches until a deep golden brown, 6–8 minutes. Using a slotted spoon, transfer the ribs to a paper towel–lined plate to drain. Serve with Green Chile Nam Jim Sauce.

Caramelized Chile Roasted Chicken

Roasted chicken with crispy skin, caramelized sticky chile sauce, something that you can hold in your fingers and devour... need I say more? Be sure to have lots of paper napkins on hand.

serves 4-6
• • • • • • • • •

preparation
10 minutes

marinating
1 hour

cooking
15 minutes

fresh

8–12 chicken drumsticks, skin on

1 quantity of Chile Tamarind Caramel (page 235)

lime wedges, to serve

spices

1 teaspoon ground cinnamon

½ teaspoon ground white pepper

½ teaspoon allspice

½ teaspoon ground coriander

½ teaspoon ground turmeric

freshly ground black pepper

pantry

1 tablespoon vegetable oil

salt

1. Use a sharp knife to score 3 deep cuts into each chicken drumstick, right down to the bone. This will ensure that the marinade gets all the way through the meat and that they cook quicker so the meat stays moist and juicy.

2. In a small bowl, mix together the cinnamon, white pepper, allspice, coriander, and turmeric with some black pepper and the oil. Place the drumsticks in a shallow dish and pour over the marinade. Cover the dish with plastic wrap and marinate the drumsticks in the refrigerator for at least 1 hour.

3. Preheat the oven to 400°F.

4. Line a roasting pan with parchment paper and place the chicken on top. Season with salt and roast in the oven until three-quarters cooked, about 10 minutes.

5. Remove the chicken from the oven and pour over half the Chile Tamarind Caramel. Return to the oven to roast for another 5 minutes.

6. When the drumsticks are caramelized, roasted, and delicious, serve with lime wedges and the remaining Chile Tamarind Caramel for dipping.

Fish & Seafood

chapter 4

Spice-fried Squid

preparation
15 minutes

soaking
1 hour

cooking
1 minute

Squid, shrimp, and other sweet seafood lend themselves very well to being fried with a hot and salty coating. It could be salt and pepper or salt and chile or a combination of crushed pepper, red pepper flakes, and Sichuan pepper – they are all excellent options and make a great snack.

fresh

1 lb squid

⅔ cup milk, for soaking

2-inch piece of ginger, peeled and grated

1 red chile, seeded and finely chopped

pantry

3 tablespoons rice flour

3 teaspoons Salt & Pepper Mix (page 246)

vegetable oil, for deep-frying

to serve

roughly chopped cilantro leaves

lime wedges

1. Score the inside of the squid with a crisscross pattern, running the knife from side to side, making sure that you do not cut all the way through. Then cut into 1¼-by-2-inch pieces.

2. Soak the squid in the milk for at least 1 hour to tenderize. When ready to cook, remove the squid from the milk and pat dry with paper towels.

3. In a large bowl, combine the ginger, red chile, rice flour, and Salt & Pepper Mix mix well. Add the squid to the bowl and stir to make sure the pieces are fully coated.

4. Fill a wok one-quarter full with vegetable oil and heat over medium-high heat until it registers 350°F on a deep-frying thermometer. Shake off any excess flour from the squid pieces, then carefully add them to the hot oil. Cook for 1 minute, then remove with a slotted spoon and drain well on paper towels. Serve garnished with cilantro and lime wedges.

* how to *
PREPARE SQUID

* *Pull out the tentacles, then pull off the side flaps of the squid. The squid tubes have a natural seam that runs down one side. Use a sharp knife to split them open and scrape off any jelly-like substance and discard.*

* *Remove the outer skin from the squid and discard.*

* *With the tentacles, take your thumb and finger in front of the ink sack and push toward the tentacles. There is a small hard beak that will be exposed, remove this and discard, then cut between the ink sack and the tentacles. You will be left with the opened-out tubes and the tentacles. Wash them in cold running water, then pat dry with paper towels.*

CHEF'S TIP

If you don't have a deep-frying thermometer, fry a small piece of bread – if the oil is ready, the bread should turn golden in about 15 seconds.

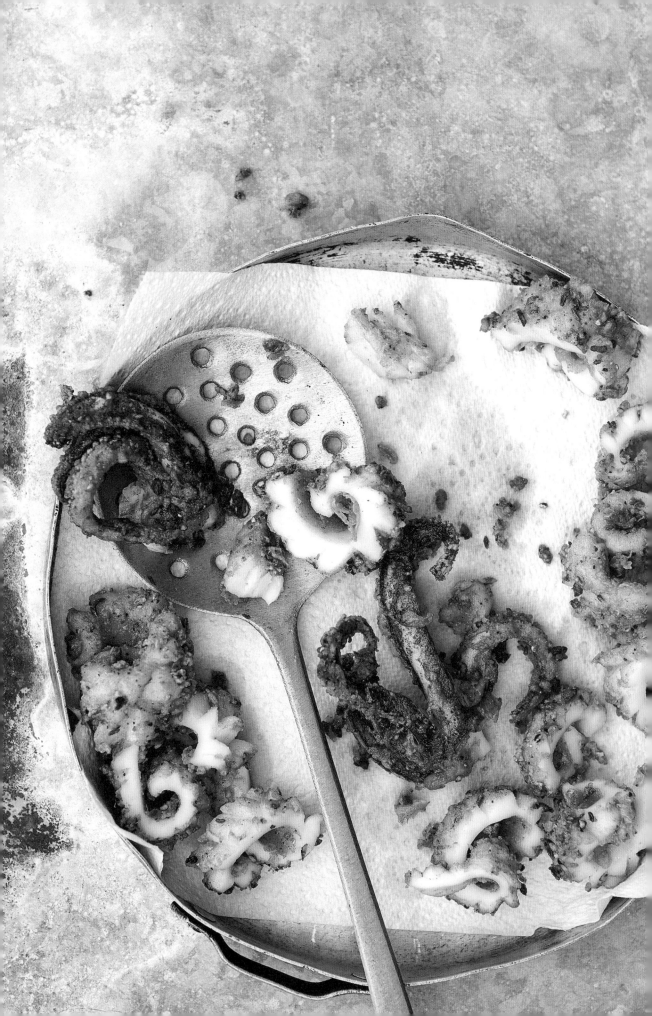

serves 4-6
• • • • • • • •

preparation
10 minutes

cooking
1–2 minutes

Grilled Scallops
with green cashew nut relish

The bright green of this sauce is very vivid, and the sauce is a great combination of different flavors and textures.

fresh

1 garlic clove

2 pieces of ginger, each 1½-inches, peeled

4 medium-hot green chiles, seeded and finely chopped

large bunch of cilantro, leaves and stems roughly chopped, plus 3 extra sprigs, leaves picked and chopped, for garnish

juice of 2 limes

18 scallops (find the largest scallops you can)

3 spring onions, finely chopped

spices

freshly ground black pepper

pantry

2 tablespoons blanched skinless cashew nuts, toasted

2 tablespoons blanched skinless peanuts, toasted

½ teaspoon superfine sugar

½ teaspoon salt, plus more to taste

3 tablespoons coconut cream

2 tablespoons vegetable oil

to serve

12–18 scallop shells, cleaned (optional)

1. Set aside half the nuts to garnish the finished dish. Place the remaining nuts in a food processor and add the garlic, 1 piece of ginger and the sugar and salt and process to a paste. Add the green chile and chopped cilantro and blend again. Add the coconut cream and 2 tablespoons water and blend together; don't overblend the ingredients, as you want a little bit of texture.

2. Transfer the paste to a bowl and add the lime juice. Taste to check the balance of flavors and adjust the seasoning if needed.

3. Clean the scallops by removing the small opaque muscle from the side that attaches the fish to the shell. The orange-colored roe can be left on or removed, depending on your taste. Place the scallops on a few layers of paper towels to dry.

4. Meanwhile, finely slice the remaining piece of ginger, stack the slices, and finely cut into thin matchsticks. Crush the reserved nuts.

5. Preheat a grill or grill pan to hot. When the scallops are dry, season them with salt and black pepper. Oil the grill and grill the scallops for 60–80 seconds on each side depending on the thickness of the scallops. To turn the scallops quickly, use two dessert spoons, one in each hand, and flick the scallops over from one spoon to the other. When the scallops are grilled on both sides, remove from the grill.

6. Place 1 scallop in each shell (if using). Spoon over a little cashew relish, sprinkle with some ginger matchsticks and spring onions, then some crushed nuts and cilantro leaves. Serve immediately.

* THAI *
knife techniques

Many of the ingredients in Thai cooking are very pungent or aromatic, are often eaten raw in the form of a garnish, and can often be fibrous, tough, or woody. This means that you have to chop a lot of these ingredients finely. A large, sharp cook's knife and the techniques described below are essential.

GINGER

When choosing ginger, select the most fresh looking and juicy. If the outside is dry and bark-like, then the flesh inside is going to be tough and woody. Always buy more ginger than you need because it keeps well and you never know what the inside is really like, so you may need some more.

Use a large, sharp cook's knife. Peel the ginger, cutting away the peel and straightening the edges (keep all the trimmings as you can use them for curry pastes).

Cut the ginger into thin slices, aiming to get them as thin as possible.

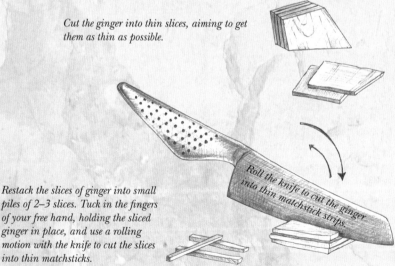

Restack the slices of ginger into small piles of 2–3 slices. Tuck in the fingers of your free hand, holding the sliced ginger in place, and use a rolling motion with the knife to cut the slices into thin matchsticks.

Roll the knife to cut the ginger into thin matchstick strips.

Ginger matchsticks are visually appealing and can be used to garnish salads and curries. You can also grate ginger, but it will not look quite as nice.

FRESH LIME LEAVES

It is important to cut fresh lime leaves very finely, because they are not palatable in large chunks. This technique is used again and again in Thai cooking. If lime leaves are not available, use fresh lime zest, which provides some of the aromatic qualities of finely sliced lime leaves.

On the back of the lime leaves there is a raised stem. Use a sharp knife to shave the stem from the leaf so that the leaves are flat.

Tightly roll the leaves into a thin, firm cigar shape. Working the knife rhythmically with a rolling motion, finely shred the leaves into thin needle-like threads, aiming to get them as fine as possible.

CHILES

The seeds and white membrane are the hottest parts of the chile. If you remove them, you have a bit more control over the heat of the chile.

To seed long red or green chiles, first cut the tops off and discard.

Hold the knife horizontally to the board at the top of the chile and place your free hand lightly on top the chile. Carefully move the knife through the center of the chile, using the whole of the blade from the tip, cutting the chile in half.

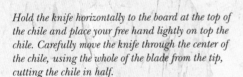

When the chile is halved, run the knife from the tip of the chile to the base, repeating the exaggerated sawing motion and slicing out all the seeds and white membrane. Discard the seeds and membrane and wash the cutting board.

Group 2–3 halves of chile, interior flesh facing up, and finely slice with a rolling motion of the knife.

serves 4
• • • •

preparation
5 minutes

marinating
10 minutes

cooking
6 minutes

fresh

4 cilantro roots, cleaned and
finely chopped

1 red chile, seeded and finely
chopped

1½-inch piece of ginger, peeled
and grated

juice of 1 lime

4 fillets of fish, such as sea bream,
snapper, sea mullet, or rainbow
trout, skin on

1 quantity of Chile Tamarind
Caramel (page 235)

2 cilantro sprigs, leaves picked,
for garnish

spices

freshly ground black pepper

pantry

salt

2 tablespoons flaked coconut,
toasted

Grilled Fish

with chile tamarind caramel

This intense rich caramel goes very well
with the sweet taste of the fish.

1. Using a mortar and pestle, grind the cilantro roots with the red
chile and a pinch of salt. Add the ginger and the lime juice and
grind together to a paste.

2. Place the fish fillets in a shallow dish and spread the paste over
them. Cover the dish with plastic wrap and marinate the fish in the
refrigerator for 10 minutes.

3. Preheat a grill, grill pan, or broiler to hot. Season the marinated
fish with salt and pepper. If using a grill pan, cook the fish, skin side
down first. If using a broiler, cook the fish skin side up. Grill for
3 minutes on each side, then transfer to a serving platter, placing
the fish on the platter skin side up, which should be blistered and
golden brown.

4. Spoon over some of the Tamarind Chile Caramel and garnish
with the coconut and cilantro leaves.

serves 4
●●●●

preparation
10 minutes

cooking
3 minutes

Sesame-seared Tuna
with lemongrass & ginger

This fantastic marinade is packed with flavor, color, and texture and works brilliantly with seared tuna.

fresh
1¼-inch piece of ginger, peeled and grated

2 lemongrass stalks, finely sliced

grated zest and juice of 3 limes

grated zest and juice of 1 orange

4 spring onions, finely sliced

2 green chiles, seeded and finely chopped

1 lb tuna, cut into 4 steaks

10 mint leaves, finely chopped

3 cilantro sprigs, leaves picked and roughly chopped

spices
freshly ground black pepper

pantry
2 tablespoons light soy sauce

3 tablespoons sesame seeds

1 tablespoon vegetable oil

salt

1. In a medium bowl, mix together the ginger, lemongrass, lime and orange zest and juice, soy sauce, spring onions, and chiles.

2. Season the tuna steaks with salt and black pepper and sprinkle with the sesame seeds.

3. Heat a frying pan over high heat until hot. When hot, add the vegetable oil. Sear the tuna steaks for 90 seconds on each side.

4. Remove the tuna steaks from the pan and place them in the marinade. Mix in half the mint and cilantro.

5. Serve the tuna with the marinade spooned over the top of the fish and garnish with remaining mint and cilantro.

CHEF'S TIP

Make sure that your tuna is a sustainable tuna, such as albacore or skipjack or a smaller species of tuna.

Crispy Fried Whitebait
with Thai spices

serves 4
••••

preparation
5 minutes

marinating
5 minutes

cooking
3 minutes
(per batch)

Whitebait are small fish that you deep-fry whole. They are the perfect snack or starter to any meal. You can also use fresh anchovies or sardines.

fresh

1 lb whitebait, cleaned

juice of 1 lime

2 lemongrass stalks, finely chopped

1½-inch piece of ginger, peeled and grated

pantry

¾ cup vegetable oil

1 tablespoon fish sauce

3 teaspoons Salt & Pepper Mix (page 246)

¾ cup rice flour

to serve

handful of torn cilantro leaves

lime wedges

Hot & Sour Red Chile Sauce (page 234), Fresh Chile Jam (page 239), or Green Chile Nam Jim Sauce (page 237)

1. Preheat the vegetable oil in a wok to 400°F or until a cube of bread dropped in browns in 15 seconds.

2. Put the whitebait in a bowl with the lime juice and fish sauce. Add the lemongrass, ginger, and Salt & Pepper Mix and mix to ensure all the whitebait are coated. Let sit for 5 minutes to absorb all the flavors.

3. Put the rice flour in a shallow dish or on a plate and dip the whitebait into the flour, shaking off any excess. Make sure the fish are coated with flour, then place them in a sieve to shake off any excess flour.

4. When the oil is hot, deep-fry the whitebait in small batches until golden brown, about 3 minutes. Drain the fried fish on paper towels. To serve, garnish with cilantro and serve with lime wedges and Hot & Sour Red Chile Sauce, Fresh Chile Jam, or Green Chile Nam Jim Sauce.

CHEF'S TIP

This marinade can be used for other fish and shellfish, such as shrimp and squid.

Turmeric Grilled Fish

serves 4-6

• • • • • • • • •

preparation
20 minutes

marinating
20 minutes

cooking
9–10 minutes

You can use any small- to medium-size fish for this dish, allowing one fish per person. Alternatively, you could use a large whole fish for a number of people.

fresh

2 limes, plus more lime wedges to serve

4 red chiles, seeded

2 lemongrass stalks, tough outer leaves removed and stems finely chopped

1½-inch piece of ginger, peeled and grated

4 shallots, chopped

1 whole fish, such as sea bream, sea bass, or snapper, weighing about 2 lb, cleaned (or 4–6 smaller fish if preferred)

spices

1 teaspoon ground turmeric

pantry

1 teaspoon salt

¾ cup coconut cream

1. Use a sharp knife to cut off the skin and pith from the limes, then finely chop the flesh.

2. Using a mortar and pestle, grind the chiles and salt together. Add the lemongrass and ginger and work into a paste. Add the shallots and lime flesh, then add a little of the coconut cream to bring the paste together.

3. Transfer the marinade to a wide bowl, add the remaining coconut cream and the turmeric and mix together.

4. Cut 3 diagonal slits in each side of the fish, cutting down to the bone to allow the marinade to penetrate into the center. Add the fish to the marinade and turn so that the whole fish is well coated. Cover the bowl with plastic wrap and marinate the fish in the refrigerator for 20 minutes, turning occasionally so that the fish is evenly coated.

5. Preheat a grill or grill pan until hot. Fold a large piece of foil in half and lay it on the grill. Place the fish on the foil and grill until browned and cooked, 5–6 minutes on each side, basting frequently with any leftover marinade.

6. Serve immediately with lime wedges as a snack, starter, or as part of larger Asian meal.

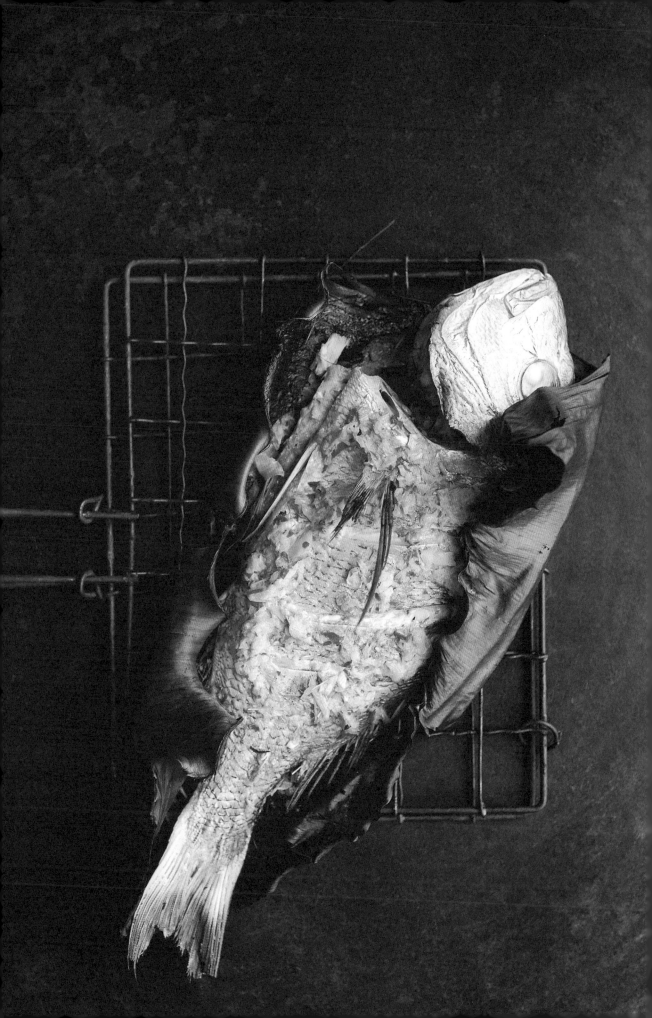

Miang Pla Thuu
Thai salad of mackerel with ginger, shallots & lime

serves 6
● ● ● ● ● ●

preparation
10 minutes

cooking
6 minutes

Any oily fish that has a sweet taste can be used for this simple salad. The flavors are quite intense, so it is best eaten as an appetizer.

fresh
1½ lb fish fillets, such as mackerel, members of the tuna family, swordish, kingfish, or rainbow trout, skin on

2 limes

2 medium-hot green chiles, seeded and finely chopped

1½-inch piece of ginger, peeled and grated

4 shallots, finely sliced

crisp lettuce leaves, to serve (optional)

spices
freshly ground black pepper

pantry
salt

vegetable oil, for cooking

2 tablespoons fish sauce

2 teaspoons golden brown sugar

½ cup blanched skinless peanuts, toasted and crushed

1. Heat a heavy-bottomed frying pan over medium-high heat. Season the fish with salt and black pepper. Add a little oil to the pan and cook the fish, skin side down, for 3 minutes. Turn the fish over and cook until the flesh is golden brown and cooked, about 3 minutes. You may need to cook for longer depending on the cut of fish. Remove the fish and let cool.

2. Zest one of the limes, set aside the zest, then use a sharp knife to remove the white pith from the lime and discard. Cut the flesh of the lime into thin slices, removing any thick white pieces of membrane. Juice the remaining lime into a large bowl and mix with the fish sauce and brown sugar to make a sauce.

3. Flake the fish into the sauce, removing any bones or pieces of skin as you go. Add the chiles, diced lime, ginger, shallots, and lime zest and gently mix together to avoid breaking the fish into a pulp. Taste the mixture and adjust accordingly – it should be hot, sweet, salty, and sour. Mix in the crushed peanuts and serve on individual plates or, if using, spoon the mixture into the lettuce leaves and serve.

Stir-fried Cod
with sugar snap peas, ginger & five-spice powder

serves 4
● ● ● ●
(as part of a
large meal)

preparation
10 minutes

cooking
8 minutes

This is a simple stir-fry that is packed full of flavor. Stir-fries from China and Southeast Asia often feature a couple of prominent ingredients, such as ginger and chile.

fresh

1½-inch piece of ginger, peeled and cut into thin slices

½ lb sugar snap peas, trimmed

2 garlic cloves, finely chopped

3 cilantro roots, cleaned and finely chopped

1 red chile, seeded and finely chopped

1¼ lb cod (or other firm white flesh fish, such as ling), cut into ¾-inch cubes

4 spring onions, finely chopped

juice of 1 lime

3 cilantro sprigs, leaves picked

spices

freshly ground black pepper

1 teaspoon five-spice powder

½ teaspoon ground coriander

½ teaspoon ground cinnamon

pantry

salt

2 tablespoons vegetable oil

1½ tablespoons fish sauce

1 tablespoon soy sauce

1. Heat a wok over medium-high heat. Add 1 tablespoon of the oil and fry the ginger for 1 minute until fragrant. Add the sugar snap peas, spreading them around the wok so that they are in contact with the heat. Fry for 2 minutes, season with salt and black pepper, then use a slotted spoon to remove the ginger and snap peas from the wok.

2. Add the remaining oil to the wok and fry the garlic, cilantro roots, and chile until fragrant, about 1 minute, then add the fish. Season with the five-spice powder, coriander, and cinnamon and cook until the fish has browned, about 2 minutes. Add the fish sauce and soy sauce and stir-fry until bubbling.

3. Return the ginger and snap peas to the wok, add the spring onions, and mix together. Transfer to plates, squeeze over the lime juice, garnish with cilantro leaves, and serve.

Aromatic Smoked Fish

This is a simple way of transforming the flavor of a delicate fish. Other fish or shellfish can be used, with oily ones, such as mackerel, salmon, trout, tuna, or shrimp, being the best choice.

serves 4-6
● ● ● ● ● ● ● ● ●

preparation
15 minutes

marinating
20 minutes

smoking
12–15 minutes

fresh
juice of 1 lime

1 lb fish (oily fish, such as mackerel, rainbow trout, salmon, or sea mullet are good, but any fish fillet will work)

2 lemongrass stalks, roughly chopped

1½–2-inch piece of ginger, peeled and roughly chopped

spices
freshly ground black pepper

4 star anise

4 cinnamon sticks

1 tablespoon fennel seeds, crushed

1 tablespoon coriander seeds, crushed

pantry
3–4 tablespoons golden brown sugar

2 tablespoons light soy sauce

½ cup uncooked white Thai rice

2 oz jasmine tea or green tea (teabags are fine)

1 cup desiccated coconut

1. Combine 2 teaspoons of the brown sugar, soy sauce, lime juice, and some black pepper in a shallow dish. Add the fish fillets and turn them so they are coated. Cover the dish with plastic wrap and marinate the fish in the refrigerator for about 20 minutes.

2. Line a large wok with two layers of foil. Mix all the remaining ingredients together in a bowl, then place them on the foil in the center of the wok. Set a wire rack on top of the foil.

3. Place the fillets on the rack and cover with a lid.

4. Start the heat on medium-high so that the smoking mix begins to caramelize for 2 minutes, then turn down the heat. Smoke the fish for 12–15 minutes, turning once while smoking. When cooked, remove the fish and let cool. When the fish is cool, remove the skin, bones, and gray blood line and serve.

5. The smoked fish will keep for about 3 days in the refrigerator.

CHEF'S TIP

The fish or shellfish can be smoked a couple of days in advance, and it can be used for salads or other dishes. If you are using a larger fish, it may take a little longer to smoke and cook.

MY

THAI

COOKBOOK

TOM KIME

PHOTOGRAPHS BY LISA LINDER

weldon**owen**

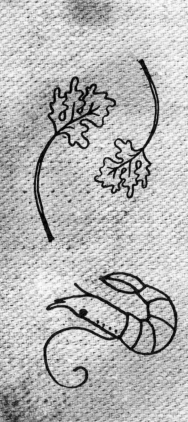

Contents

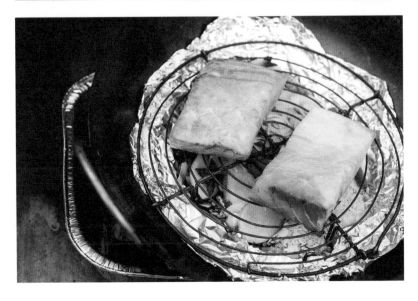

serves 4

● ● ● ●

(as a starter)

preparation
10 minutes

cooking
10 minutes

Tea-smoked Trout
with toasted coconut & ginger

Fillets of rainbow trout are great for smoking with an aromatic smoking mix because the fish has a good oil content. The smoking imparts a beautiful aroma to the fish.

fresh

4 Aromatic Smoked Fish fillets (page 138; I use rainbow trout or salmon)

1½-inch piece of ginger peeled and grated

1 red chile, seeded and finely chopped

1 quantity of Fresh Chile Jam (page 239)

2 mint sprigs, leaves picked

juice of 2 limes

spices

1 tablespoon coriander seeds, crushed

pantry

½ cup dried flaked coconut

1. Smoke the fish fillets with the smoking mix for about 10 minutes as instructed on page 138.

2. Meanwhile, add the coconut, coriander, ginger, and red chile to a dry pan. Cook slowly over medium heat until the coconut and coriander are toasted, fragrant, and golden brown, about 4 minutes. The ginger and chile will dry out and become fragrant.

3. Flake the smoked fish into large chunks and arrange them on individual plates or a large platter.

4. Dash some Chile Jam over the fish. Tear the mint leaves and add them to the fried mixture. Scatter the coconut, ginger, and mint garnish over the top and squeeze over the lime juice. Serve straightaway.

preparation
10 minutes

cooking
1 minute

Grilled Tuna
with Asian herb sauce

Serve these little chunks of tuna as an appetizer with cold drinks before a meal or as one of the starter courses.

fresh

2 red chiles, seeded and finely chopped

2 spring onions, finely chopped

grated zest and juice of 2 limes

1 lb tuna, cut into 3 steaks

2 cilantro sprigs, leaves picked

2 Thai basil sprigs, leaves picked (or regular basil)

pantry

1 tablespoon coriander seeds

¼ teaspoon ground black pepper, plus more for seasoning

to serve

salt

2 tablespoons fish sauce

2 teaspoons sesame oil

vegetable oil, for frying

1. Toast the coriander seeds in a frying pan over medium heat, then roughly crush them using a mortar and pestle.

2. Combine all the ingredients, except for the tuna and herbs, in a bowl and mix well to make a sauce. Set aside.

3. Add a little vegetable oil to a nonstick frying pan and heat over high heat.

4. Season the tuna with salt and black pepper. Sear the tuna for 40 seconds on each of the 4 sides, turning the tuna chunks using tongs.

5. Remove the tuna from the pan and set on a cutting board. Use a serrated bread knife to slice the tuna into thin slices, then arrange them on a large platter.

6. Spoon over the sauce and tear the cilantro and basil leaves over the top to finish.

Marinated Shrimp Satay

Shrimp paste, used in this dish, is available at Asian markets. It has a strong pungent smell when raw; however, when you cook the paste it loses its pungency and becomes more aromatic.

serves 4-6

• • • • • • • •

preparation
10 minutes

marinating
1 hour

cooking
10 minutes

fresh

2 garlic cloves, finely chopped

2 lemongrass stalks, tough outer leaves removed and stalks finely chopped

juice of 1 lime, plus more lime wedges to serve

2 lb large raw shrimp, peeled and deveined

spice

½ teaspoon red pepper flakes

pantry

2 tablespoons blanched skinless peanuts

pinch of salt

1 tablespoon vegetable oil

1 teaspoon shrimp paste
(see page 18)

6 tablespoons coconut cream

1 packet of 6-inch bamboo skewers, soaked in cold water for 30 minutes

I. Toast the peanuts in a pan over medium-high heat until golden brown, stirring the peanuts constantly so that they do not burn. Transfer them to a mortar and use a pestle and grind to a fine texture.

2. On a clean cutting board or using a mortar and pestle, work the garlic into a paste with the salt and red pepper flakes.

3. Heat the vegetable oil in a pan over medium-high heat. Add the garlic paste and shrimp paste and fry until fragrant and aromatic, then add the lime juice and coconut cream and stir together. Simmer gently over low heat for 4–5 minutes. Taste the mixture and adjust the seasoning if needed – it should be hot, sweet, and salty and cut with the sourness of the lime. Transfer to a shallow dish and let cool.

4. Once the paste has cooled, add the shrimp. Cover the dish with plastic wrap and marinate the fish in the refrigerator for at least 1 hour.

5. Preheat a broiler or grill to hot. Thread 3–4 marinated shrimp onto the soaked bamboo skewers. Grill the skewers under a hot broiler or on a grill for a couple of minutes on each side, then serve with lime wedges.

CHEF'S TIP

You could use other types of shellfish, squid, or cubes of fish for this recipe.

Stir-fried Mussels & Clams
with chile jam

With only a few ingredients, this is a very simple dish to prepare, and the flavors are delicious. It's the sort of dish that encourages you to roll up your sleeves and dive in. You could use clams or mussels or a combination of the two.

serves 4
••••

preparation
15 minutes

cooking
6 minutes

fresh

1¾ lb mussels, cleaned and debearded (or other seafood)

¾ lb clams, cleaned

1¼-inch piece of ginger, peeled and finely sliced

2 lemongrass stalks, outer leaves discarded and stems finely chopped

4 tablespoons Fresh Chile Jam (page 239)

a small bunch of Thai basil, leaves picked and washed

juice of 2 limes

spices

freshly ground black pepper

pantry

2 tablespoons vegetable oil

salt

1. Prepare the mussels and clams (see box below).

2. Heat a heavy-bottomed pan or wok over medium-high heat. Add the oil and fry half the ginger and lemongrass for 1–2 minutes until fragrant and aromatic. Add the Chile Jam, mussels, and clams and cook over high heat, stirring to coat with the jam.

3. Add 6 tablespoons water, cover with a lid and cook over high heat, shaking the pan every now and again, for 2 minutes. Remove the lid and stir from the bottom. Replace the lid and cook for another 2 minutes until all the mussels and clams have opened.

4. Add half the basil and lime juice and season with plenty of black pepper. Taste the juice and adjust the seasoning if needed – it may need a little salt. Mix together and serve in bowls with the juice poured over the top. Garnish with the remaining basil, lemongrass, and ginger.

---

* how to *
PREPARE SHELLFISH

* Wash the mussels (or other shellfish) in plenty of cold running water. Remove any dirt or barnacles with an old knife.

* De-beard the mussels and then wash until the water is completely clear.

* Discard any mussels that do not close when you tap them— they're dead and shouldn't be cooked, and also discard any that smell.

serves 4-6
• • • • • • • • •

preparation
15 minutes

marinating
10 minutes

cooking
10 minutes

fresh

5 red chiles, seeded and finely
chopped

2 garlic cloves, finely chopped

1½-inch piece of ginger, peeled
and finely chopped

4 cilantro sprigs, leaves picked
and finely chopped and stems
reserved

juice of 3 limes

1 large white-fleshed fish (round
or flat – a sea bream or an ocean
perch is perfect)

4 lemongrass stalks, finely
chopped

spices

½ teaspoon freshly ground
white pepper

pantry

pinch of salt

2 tablespoons fish sauce

1 teaspoon superfine sugar

Grilled Fish
with chile, garlic & ginger

The cuisine of Southern Thailand is famous
for its great seafood dishes and its almost
compulsory use of fiery red chiles, but you
can tone down the level of heat in this dish
if you prefer.

1. Using a mortar and pestle, grind the chiles and garlic together.
Add a little salt to work as an abrasive and help break down the
fibrous spices. Add the ginger and cilantro stems and work into a
paste. Add 1 tablespoon of the fish sauce, the juice of 1 of the limes,
and a splash of water and grind a bit more.

2. Cut 4 diagonal slashes on each side of the fish, cutting down
to the bone. Place the fish in a shallow dish, and rub the chile paste
into the slashes on both sides, making sure the fish is well covered.
Cover the dish with plastic wrap and marinate the fish in the
refrigerator for 5–10 minutes while you preheat the grill and make
the sauce.

3. Preheat a broiler, grill, or grill pan. Using a mortar and pestle,
grind the lemongrass, salt, and sugar to a coarse paste. Add the white
pepper and cilantro leaves and continue to grind until you have a
semi-smooth paste. Add the remaining fish sauce and lime juice and
mix until well blended. Add ¼ cup water and combine.

4. If using grill, you will need a thin metal grill basket. If using
an broiler, you will need a shallow pan lined with foil. Arrange
the fish for the style of cooking you're using. Cook the fish for
4–5 minutes on each side, depending on the weight. Be careful
when you turn them over so that the skin does not tear.

5. When the fish is cooked, arrange it on a large platter and splash
the lemongrass and pepper sauce over the top.

Cutting slashes in the fish allows
the spice paste to permeate the
flesh and the heat to penetrate to
the bone, caramelizing the fish.

curries & soups

chapter 5

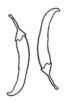

Coconut Fish Curry

serves 4-6
• • • • • • • • • •

preparation
15 minutes

cooking
25 minutes

You can use any combination of fish or shellfish for this dish, but make sure the end result always has a balance of hot, sweet, salt, and sour.

fresh

5 garlic cloves

3 small red onions, chopped

1¼-inch piece of ginger, peeled

2 lemongrass stalks, tough outer leaves removed and stalks chopped

grated zest of 1 lime

3 lime leaves

juice of 2 limes

¾ lb firm white-fleshed fish, cut into ¾-inch cubes

½ lb large raw shrimp, peeled and deveined

½ lb cooked crabmeat, picked over (or squid, scored; or another fish or shellfish of your choice)

3 cilantro sprigs, leaves picked

3 mint sprigs, leaves picked

spices

6 dried red chiles, cut in half and soaked in warm water until softened

1 teaspoon ground turmeric

freshly ground black pepper

pantry

1 teaspoon salt, plus more for seasoning

1 tablespoon vegetable oil

2 teaspoons shrimp paste (see page 18)

2¾ cups coconut cream

1 tablespoon fish sauce

1 tablespoon tamarind paste

1. Place the softened chiles in a food processor or blender with the garlic, red onions, ginger, lemongrass, lime zest, and salt and purée to a smooth paste.

2. Heat a heavy-bottomed pan over medium heat and add a little oil. Fry the shrimp paste for 2 minutes until fragrant and aromatic, then add the puréed ingredients.

3. Add the turmeric and lime leaves and cook the paste slowly for about 10 minutes. Add the coconut cream and cook until it has reduced by one-third. Taste to check the balance of flavors and adjust if needed.

4. Add the lime juice, fish sauce, and tamarind paste. Season the fish with salt and black pepper and add it to the simmering curry. Turn off the heat and let sit for 2 minutes.

5. Add the shrimp and cook for 1 minute, then add the crabmeat. Stir the fish so that it is all coated in the curry, but do not let it boil, as the fish will break up.

6. Tear the cilantro and mint leaves into the curry. Taste one more time and add more lime or fish sauce if necessary, and serve with rice or noodles.

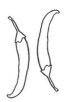

Thai Green Curry
with shrimp

serves 4-6
• • • • • • • • •

preparation
10 minutes

cooking
10 minutes

The best way to make a really good curry is to make a big batch, then you can freeze the curry paste in small containers so that you can pull out a stunning curry whenever you want.

fresh

1 portion of Green Curry Paste (page 224)

2 lemongrass stalks, tough outer leaves removed and stalks finely sliced

⅓ lb green beans, trimmed (snow peas or asparagus can also be used)

juice of 2 limes

juice of 1 orange

1 lb large raw shrimp, peeled and deveined

3 cilantro sprigs, leaves picked

2 Thai basil sprigs, leaves picked

2 long green chiles, seeded and finely chopped

3 spring onions, finely chopped

pantry

1¼ cups coconut cream

1 tablespoon tamarind paste

1 tablespoon fish sauce

1. Heat the curry paste in a saucepan over medium heat until just steaming. Add half the coconut cream and bring to a boil (add more cream later if needed).

2. Add half the lemongrass and simmer gently over a low heat, stirring occasionally to prevent it from sticking. Thin the sauce if necessary with a little water.

3. Add the green beans and simmer for 2 minutes. Reduce the sauce by simmering for another 3 minutes.

4. Add the tamarind paste, juice of one of the limes, the orange juice and fish sauce and stir together. Add the shrimp and continue simmering.

5. Roughly chop the cilantro and basil leaves and stir about one-third into the sauce. Taste the sauce to check the balance of flavors and adjust if needed to get a balance of hot, sour, salty, and sweet. Garnish the finished curry with the remaining lemongrass, cilantro and basil leaves, and the green chiles and spring onions. Serve with rice or noodles.

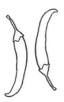

Red Curry
with chicken

serves 4-6
• • • • • • • •

preparation
5 minutes

cooking
10 minutes

This is one of my favorite curries, because it has everything in one mouthful: roasted meat, spices, heat, herbs, and the sourness of pineapple and tamarind—an exquisite combination of flavors.

fresh

1 garlic clove, finely chopped

1 portion of Red Curry Paste (page 223)

3 grilled skinless and boneless chicken breasts

½ a fresh pineapple, peeled and cut into chunks

6 cherry tomatoes, halved

4 Thai basil sprigs (or regular basil)

pantry

2 tablespoons vegetable oil

1 cup coconut cream

1 tablespoon fish sauce

1 teaspoon grated palm sugar

to serve

1 large red chile, seeded and finely chopped

1¼-inch piece of ginger, peeled and finely sliced into matchsticks

1. Heat the oil in a heavy-bottomed pan over medium-high heat. Sauté the garlic until golden brown, then stir in the curry paste and heat through. Add the coconut cream, stirring all the time, and bring to a boil.

2. Reduce the heat and add the fish sauce and palm sugar and simmer for 5 minutes.

3. Add the grilled chicken and turn to coat in the sauce. Add the pineapple and tomatoes and stir in the basil. Garnish with chopped red chile and ginger and serve with rice or noodles.

• 6 ways with •
COCONUT & COCONUT MILK

❶ Steamed Mussels & Shrimp

Heat a splash of oil, add 1 lb cleaned mussels and 2 tablespoons red curry paste.

Add 5 lime leaves and 2 chopped lemongrass stalks.

Stir in ¾ cup coconut cream.

Bring to a boil with 3 tablespoons fish sauce and the juice of 1 lemon.

Add ½ lb raw peeled shrimp. Cover and cook for 2 minutes until the shrimp are cooked and the mussels have opened.

Tear a handful of cilantro leaves into the mussels and serve with lime wedges.

❷ Coconut Cream Pudding

Simmer ¾ cup heavy cream, ¼ teaspoon agar powder, and 3 tablespoons superfine sugar in a saucepan. Stir to dissolve the sugar.

Remove from the heat and stir in 6 tablespoons coconut cream.

Pour into 2-cup ramekins and place in the refrigerator for 2 hours to set.

Toast ½ lb desiccated coconut in a frying pan until golden.

Add 1 teaspoon ground cinnamon, ½ teaspoon ground nutmeg, and ¼ teaspoon ground cardamom and cook until fragrant.

Zest 1 lemon and 1 orange and add to the coconut.

Turn out the puddings, scatter the coconut over the top, and drizzle with honey.

❸ Turmeric & Coconut Fried Fish

Mix together a peeled, grated 1¼-inch piece of ginger, 2 chopped red chiles, ¼ cup rice flour, 6 tablespoons coconut cream, 2 eggs, 1 teaspoon ground turmeric, 2 chopped spring onions, a pinch of salt, and 2 tablespoons toasted flaked coconut.

Dust ¾ lb white fish fillets with rice flour so that they are coated.

Heat some vegetable oil for deep frying in a wok or frying pan. Dip the floured fish into the batter and shake off any excess.

Fry the fish in small batches for 3–4 minutes until the batter is golden and the fish is cooked. Serve with Green Chile Nam Jim Sauce (page 237).

❹ Creamy Pumpkin Soup

Finely chop 2 garlic cloves, 2 cleaned cilantro roots, and 2 green chiles and fry in a little oil. Add ½ teaspoon ground nutmeg and ¼ teaspoon ground cloves.

Dice ¾ lb butternut squash or pumpkin into fine cubes, coat in the spices, and season with salt and pepper.

Add 2½ cups coconut milk and simmer until the pumpkin is soft. Add the juice of 2 limes and 2 tablespoons fish sauce.

Toast 3 tablespoons desiccated coconut in a frying pan until golden.

Pour the soup into bowls and garnish with the coconut and cilantro leaves.

❺ Thai Rice Salad

Put 1 lb room-temperature cooked jasmine rice in a large bowl.

Toast 3 tablespoons desiccated coconut in a frying pan until golden brown. Add the coconut to the rice, along with a handful of bean sprouts, 2 chopped spring onions, and 1 diced cucumber.

Add the leaves from 3 sprigs of mint and basil.

Mix in ½ lb cold roasted chicken or pork, torn into shreds.

Crush 2 chopped red chiles and 1 tablespoon ginger with a pinch of salt using a mortar and pestle until smooth. Add ¼ cup coconut cream, juice of 1 lime, and 2 tablespoons fish sauce.

Mix together the rice and dressing and serve with lime wedges and Hot & Sour Red Chile Sauce (page 234).

❻ Green Herb Grilled Chicken

Crush 3 cleaned cilantro roots, 1 tablespoon ginger, and 2 garlic cloves with a little salt using a mortar and pestle.

Finely chop 4 cilantro sprigs and grind them until smooth.

Combine 1 teaspoon ground coriander, a large pinch of red pepper flakes, ⅓ cup coconut cream, and 2 tablespoons fish sauce.

Marinate 8 chicken drumsticks in the coconut mixture for 1 hour.

Make a large foil package, place the chicken inside, and tightly seal the edges.

Grill the chicken package on a hot grill for about 15 minutes, turning regularly to avoid burning. When cooked, add the juice of 1 lime and scatter over some cilantro leaves.

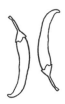

Hot & Sour Orange Curry
with grilled salmon

The fillets of salmon in this vibrant curry are grilled rare first to give them a great texture and flavor, then finished off in the curry sauce.

serves 4-6
● ● ● ● ● ● ● ● ●

preparation
5 minutes

cooking
10 minutes

fresh
1 lb salmon fillets

1 portion of Hot & Sour Orange Curry Paste (page 227)

¼ lb green beans, trimmed

a bunch of asparagus, cut into 1¼-inch lengths

1 red chile, seeded

2 lemongrass stalks, tough outer leaves removed and stalks finely chopped

3 lime leaves, finely sliced

½ a small bunch of cilantro, leaves picked

juice of 2 limes

spices
freshly ground black pepper

pantry
salt

2 tablespoons fish sauce

1. Preheat a grill pan over high heat. Season the salmon with salt and black pepper and grill the salmon fillet for 2 minutes on each side to create grill marks on the fish – you are not cooking the fish all the way through, just searing it on the outside.

2. Heat the curry paste in a medium pan over medium heat. Add the grilled fish and poach gently over a low heat for about 2 minutes, then add the green beans and asparagus and cook for another 3 minutes.

3. Add half the chile, lemongrass, and lime leaves to the pan and mix through. Serve the curry garnished with the remaining chile, lemongrass, and lime leaves and plenty of cilantro. Stir through the fish sauce and lime juice to balance the flavors. Serve with rice.

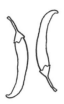

serves 4–6

●●●●●●●●●

preparation
15 minutes

cooking
3½ hours

Mussaman Curry
with spiced braised beef

This curry calls for slow cooking beef.
Cuts of meat that will work well are skirt
or flank steaks, shank, chuck steak, or top
round. Alternatively, you could use an
osso bucco–style cut. Lamb shoulder, lamb
shanks, or chicken also work well.

fresh

2 lb skirt or flank steak

1 onion, roughly chopped

2 garlic cloves

1 carrot, chopped

1 celery stalk, chopped

3 bay leaves

1¼-inch piece of ginger,
peeled and sliced

½ a long red chile, seeded

1 portion of Mussaman Curry
Paste with Toasted Peanuts
(page 228)

3 medium potatoes, peeled and
cut into ¾-inch chunks

juice of 1 lime

3 cilantro sprigs, for garnish

spices

3 cinnamon sticks

4 star anise

freshly ground black pepper

pantry

vegetable oil, for frying

salt

1¼ cups coconut cream

1 tablespoon fish sauce

1. Preheat the oven to 300°F.

2. Heat a little vegetable oil in a deep ovenproof heavy-bottomed
pot and brown the meat on all sides. Add the onion, garlic, carrot,
celery, bay leaves, ginger, and chile and continue to cook until
browned. Add the cinnamon and star anise and season with salt and
black pepper. Cover the meat with water and bring to a boil. Cover
with a lid and place in the oven until the meat is meltingly soft, at
least 3 hours. Remove from the heat and set aside.

3. When ready to make the curry, in a large pan, heat the coconut
cream with 3 tablespoons of the beef braising juices. Add the curry
paste and bring to a boil, stirring regularly to prevent the paste
from sticking. Add the potatoes and cook for about 10 minutes,
or until softened.

4. Cut the beef into 6 pieces. When the potatoes are three-quarters
cooked, add the beef to the curry. Don't break up the beef any
more as it will do that naturally as it cooks in the curry. Add another
3 tablespoons of the braising liquid.

5. Taste to check the balance of flavors and adjust if needed – it
should taste sweet, sour, and salty, with a strong toasted-spice base.

6. Add the fish sauce and lime juice to bring the flavors into
balance and highlight all the toasted spices. Garnish with cilantro
and serve with steamed rice if you like.

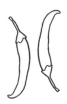

Geng Gari Curry
with roasted chicken

serves 4-6
• • • • • • • • •

preparation
10 minutes

cooking
15 minutes

A *geng gari* is a heavenly curry with a base of ground spices, which add a delicious earthy foundation to the curry. This would work really well as a vegetarian curry with roasted sweet potato and butternut squash.

fresh

½ lb chicken, cut into pieces

1 portion of Geng Gari Curry Paste (page 226)

¼ lb baby corn

juice of 2 limes

20 Thai basil leaves, roughly chopped

¾-inch piece of ginger, peeled and finely sliced into matchsticks

3 spring onions, finely sliced, for garnish

spices

1 teaspoon coriander seeds

1 teaspoon cumin seeds

freshly ground black pepper

pantry

salt

vegetable oil

1 tablespoon tamarind paste

2 tablespoons light soy sauce

1. Roughly crush the coriander and cumin seeds using a mortar and pestle. Season the chicken with salt, black pepper and the crushed spices and drizzle with oil.

2. Pan-fry or grill the chicken until golden brown and caramelized, about 10 minutes.

3. Heat the curry paste in a pan over medium heat, and add the baby corn, lime juice, tamarind, light soy sauce, and half the basil and ginger.

4. Taste the curry paste to check the balance of flavors and adjust if needed – it should be hot, sour, and salty. You could add more chile, lime, or fish sauce if needed.

5. Garnish with spring onions and the remaining basil and ginger. Serve accompanied by a crisp salad, rice, or vegetables.

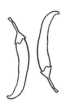

Tom Yam

hot & sour soup with roasted shallots, chicken & Thai basil

serves 4-6
• • • • • • • • •

preparation
15 minutes

cooking
35 minutes

Set out small bowls of chopped chiles, herbs, lime wedges, and light soy sauce or fish sauce so that diners can fine-tune the soup to their liking. This allows each guest to create a balance of flavors that suits their palate.

fresh

2 lemongrass stalks, chopped

1¼-inch piece of ginger, peeled and chopped

5 garlic cloves, chopped

2 red chiles, seeded and roughly chopped

4 cilantro roots, cleaned and chopped

2 cups chicken stock or broth

3 lime leaves, finely chopped

6 shallots, finely sliced

juice of 3 limes, plus more lime wedges to serve

2 grilled chicken breasts, cut into slices

2 spring onions, finely sliced

3 cilantro sprigs, leaves picked and roughly chopped

2 Thai basil sprigs (or regular basil), roughly chopped

spices

freshly ground black pepper

pantry

vegetable oil, for cooking

2 tablespoons tamarind paste

4 tablespoons fish sauce

2 teaspoons grated palm sugar

salt

1. Heat 1 tablespoon oil in a heavy-bottomed pan over medium heat. Add the lemongrass, ginger, garlic, chiles, and cilantro roots and sauté until golden brown, about 3 minutes. Add the stock, lime leaves, tamarind paste, and 2 tablespoons of fish sauce and simmer for 20 minutes.

2. Meanwhile, in a separate pan, cook the shallots in a little oil over medium-high heat with the grated palm sugar for 6–8 minutes.

3. Strain the stock through a sieve into a bowl and discard the flavoring ingredients. Pour the stock back into the pan and bring to a boil. Add the lime juice and the remaining fish sauce. Taste to check the balance of flavors and adjust if needed – it should have an underlying sweetness from the stock and caramelized vegetables.

4. When the soup is ready, place a few slices of chicken and some caramelized shallots in each bowl. Divide the spring onions, cilantro, and basil leaves among the bowls and pour the soup over. Add a squeeze of lime to each bowl and serve.

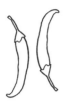

Roasted Duck Soup
with lime, chile & basil

serves 4-6
• • • • • • • • •

preparation
10 minutes

cooking
7 minutes

This is a simple yet flavorful soup with lots of lime juice, hot chiles, and zingy Thai basil. It is so refreshing and can be made with roasted chicken or roasted duck.

fresh

2 garlic cloves, finely chopped

3 small red bird's-eye chiles, bruised

3 lemongrass stalks, bruised and cut into 4 pieces

6½ cups chicken stock or broth

½ a roasted duck, skin discarded and meat shredded

juice of 3 limes

4 Thai basil sprigs (or regular basil), leaves picked and roughly chopped

pantry

1 teaspoon grated palm sugar

2 tablespoons fish sauce

salt

1. Put the garlic, chiles, palm sugar, and lemongrass in a saucepan. Add the chicken stock and bring to a boil over high heat. Reduce the heat and simmer for 5 minutes. Using a slotted spoon, remove the lemongrass pieces from the stock and discard.

2. Add the duck, fish sauce, and lime juice, stir well and taste to check the balance of flavors – it may need a little salt. Add the basil and taste again before serving, adjusting the flavors if needed.

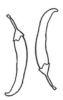

serves 4-6
• • • • • • • • •

preparation
10 minutes

cooking
15 minutes

Tom Kha Gai
chicken & coconut milk soup

This is a deliciously fragrant soup. It's more aromatic and mild and not too spicy and is typically served alongside hotter dishes to temper the heat of the meal.

fresh

2-inch piece of galangal or ginger, peeled, bruised with the back of a knife and cut into thick slices

4 lemongrass stalks, bruised with the back of knife and cut into 4–5 pieces

1 lb boneless chicken breast, cut into ¾ inch thick slices

4 small bird's-eye chiles, bruised with the back of knife

5 lime leaves, torn

juice of 2 limes

4 cilantro sprigs, leaves picked and torn

pantry

5 cups coconut milk

½ cup coconut cream

3 tablespoons fish sauce

1. Put the galangal, lemongrass, and coconut milk in a large saucepan and bring to a boil slowly, stirring regularly. Simmer gently for 5 minutes, then add the chicken and simmer for another 5 minutes until the chicken is cooked.

2. Add the coconut cream, fish sauce, chiles, lime leaves, and lime juice and bring almost to a boil, stirring, then remove from the heat. Transfer to warmed bowls and garnish with torn cilantro leaves.

Rice, Noodles & Sides

chapter 6

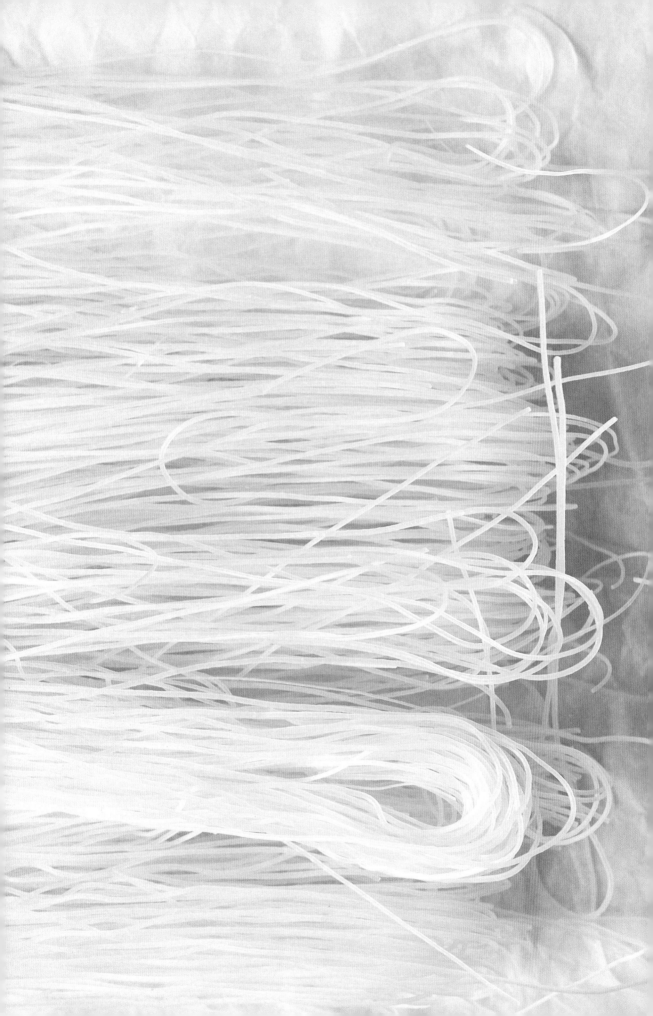

Pad Thai Fried Noodles

This is probably one of the most famous dishes in and out of Thailand and is not too challenging on the palate for anyone unfamiliar with Thai cuisine.

serves 4-6
● ● ● ● ● ● ● ● ●

preparation
10 minutes

cooking
8 minutes

fresh

¼ lb silken tofu, cut into small cubes

2 garlic cloves, finely chopped

½ lb skinless boneless chicken breast, cut into thin strips

½ lb raw shrimp, peeled, deveined and cut in half lengthwise

1 egg

juice of ½ lemon

¼ lb bean sprouts, cleaned

1 fresh red chile, seeded and finely chopped

4 spring onions, finely chopped

3 cilantro sprigs, leaves picked and torn

lemon wedges, to serve

spices

¼ teaspoon red pepper flakes

pantry

2 tablespoons vegetable oil

6 oz Sen Lek noodles (see page 17), soaked in warm water for 20 minutes until soft, then drained

2 tablespoons fish sauce

2 tablespoons blanched skinless peanuts, toasted, then crushed

1. Heat the oil in a wok over medium heat and fry the tofu until golden brown, about 3 minutes. Add the garlic and cook for 30 seconds. Add the chicken and stir-fry for 1 minute. After a minute, add the shrimp and stir well.

2. Break in the egg and stir quickly, cooking for a couple of seconds. Add the soaked noodles and stir well.

3. Mix in the lemon juice, fish sauce, and pepper flakes. Add half the bean sprouts, half the red chile. and half the spring onions. Keep stir-frying until the noodles are cooked through, about 3 minutes.

4. Turn the noodles out onto a serving platter and garnish with the remaining red chile, spring onions, and bean sprouts, and some torn cilantro leaves. Serve with lemon wedges and scatter over the peanuts.

serves 4-6
• • • • • • • • •

preparation
10 minutes

cooking
7–8 minutes

Fried Rice
with shrimp, squid & crab

This is a delicious rice dish. I use shrimp, squid, and crab here, but you could use any fish or shellfish that you like. You can also vary the level of heat and serve the rice with a spicy dipping sauce or some red pepper flakes.

fresh

1 yellow onion, finely chopped

3 garlic cloves, finely chopped

2 red chiles, seeded and finely chopped

½ lb raw shrimp, peeled, deveined and halved lengthwise

½ lb squid, cleaned and underside scored in a diamond pattern (see page 116)

2 eggs, beaten

1¾ cup cooked jasmine or fragrant rice

½ lb cooked crabmeat, picked over

juice of 2 limes

3 cilantro sprigs, leaves picked and roughly chopped

2 spring onions, finely chopped

2 basil sprigs, leaves picked

spices

freshly ground black pepper

pantry

2 tablespoons vegetable oil

3 tablespoons fish sauce

1. Heat the oil in a wok over medium heat and fry the onion until softened, 1–2 minutes. Add the garlic and chiles and fry for another minute until fragrant and aromatic.

2. Add the shrimp, stir-fry briskly for 1 minute, then add the squid and stir-fry for another minute. Add the eggs, cooking them on the upper edges of the pan so that you get a thin omelet.

3. Splash in the fish sauce, then add the cooked rice and crabmeat and continue to stir-fry for 3 minutes. Season with black pepper and lime juice.

4. Add the cilantro and spring onions and tear in the basil leaves, then quickly transfer to a large serving dish. Serve with a Green Chile Nam Jim Sauce (page 237) and sliced cucumber if you like.

serves 4-6
• • • • • • • • •

preparation
5 minutes

cooking
3 minutes

Pad Ki Mow

spicy beef noodles with lime leaves

You can use any meat and vary the ingredients and also the heat content of the dish to suit your taste. The noodles will double in weight when they are soaked.

fresh

2 garlic cloves, finely chopped

2 fresh red chiles, seeded and finely chopped

1 lb sirloin, cut into thin strips

4 lime leaves, finely sliced

2 Thai basil sprigs (or regular basil), leaves picked

spices

¼ teaspoon red pepper flakes

½ teaspoon five-spice powder

pantry

2 tablespoons vegetable oil

2 tablespoons fish sauce

½ teaspoon grated palm sugar

¼ lb Sen Yai noodles (see page 17), soaked in warm water for 20 minutes until soft, then drained

to serve

3 cilantro sprigs, leaves picked and torn

lime wedges, to serve

1. Heat the oil in a wok over medium heat. Add the garlic and fry for 1 minute until golden. Add the chiles and stir-fry for 10 seconds, then add the beef and stir-fry for about 20 seconds to seal the meat.

2. Add the fish sauce, palm sugar, lime leaves, half the basil, the pepper flakes, and the five-spice powder, stir-frying constantly.

3. Add the noodles and stir well. Continue stir-frying for about 1 minute, then taste the noodles to check that they are cooked.

4. Turn out the noodles onto a serving plate and garnish with torn cilantro leaves, the remaining basil, and the lime wedges.

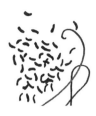

Hakka-style Fried Noodles
with pork & Thai basil

serves 4-6
••••

preparation
10 minutes

cooking
4 minutes

These noodles are quick to make and wonderfully juicy. The Thai basil gives it a fantastic licorice, aniseed taste. You can use any combination of meat and vegetables.

fresh

¾ lb pork tenderloin, cut into thin slices

2 long red chiles, seeded and finely chopped

1½-inch piece of ginger, grated

1¾ lb fresh egg noodles

1 cup chicken stock or broth

½ a bunch of garlic chives, cut into ⅜-inch lengths (available at Asian markets, but if they're unavailable, use regular chives)

½ lb bean sprouts

3 Thai basil sprigs (or regular basil), leaves picked

Hot & Sour Red Chile Sauce (page 234), to serve

spices

½ teaspoon ground white pepper

pantry

2 tablespoons vegetable oil

3 tablespoons light soy sauce

1½ tablespoons dark soy sauce

1. Heat the oil in a wok over medium heat and stir-fry the pork and red chiles for 1 minute. Add the ginger, noodles and half the stock, a little at a time, stirring to combine. Cover with a lid, turn the heat down, and simmer for 1 minute.

2. Add the light and dark soy sauce and stir-fry for 1 minute. Add a little more stock if the noodles are sticking.

3. Season with white pepper, add the garlic chives and bean sprouts, stirring all the time, then taste the noodles to check the balance of flavors and adjust if needed. Add the basil and serve with the Hot & Sour Chile Sauce.

· 6 ways with ·

GINGER & GARLIC

 Ginger, Mint & Shrimp Salad

Grind 1 tablespoon ginger peelings using a mortar and pestle until it is a smooth pulp, about 2 minutes. Using a spoon, transfer the pulp to a bowl.

Add 20 mint leaves, ½ teaspoon superfine sugar, and ½ teaspoon salt to the mortar and grind to a smooth green paste.

Juice 2 limes into the paste and add 2 chopped red chiles.

Add the juice from the ginger pulp by squeezing it into the mortar from the palm of your hand, wringing out all the juice.

Mix everything together and then pour over ½ lb cooked shrimp and garnish with the leaves from 3 sprigs of cilantro.

 Grilled Fish with Garlic, Pepper & Chile Dressing

Crush 2 garlic cloves with a little salt to a paste using a mortar and pestle.

Chop 3 seeded green chiles and 2 cilantro roots and mix with the garlic paste along with the juice of 2 lemons and 2 tablespoons fish sauce.

Rub half of the mixture onto 4 fish fillets (such as sardines or red mullet). Preheat a grill or broiler to hot and cook the fish for 3 minutes on each side.

Stir 1 teaspoon grated palm sugar or golden brown sugar to the remaining dressing along with ½ teaspoon crushed white pepper.

Serve the fish with the dressing poured over the top.

 Crisp Cucumber & Chicken Salad with Ginger

Grind 1 garlic clove, 1 seeded and chopped red chile, ½ teaspoon salt, and ½ teaspoon superfine sugar using a mortar and pestle until smooth. Add the juice of 1 orange and 2 limes.

Peel and grate a 1½-inch piece of ginger, slice 3 spring onions, and seed 1 cucumber and cut into 1½-inch batons.

Shred the meat from half a roasted chicken and mix with the cucumber.

Pick the leaves from 3 sprigs of cilantro and finely shred them.

Combine all the ingredients except for the cucumber together for the salad and dressing and pour it over the chicken and cucumber.

 Peppered Chicken with Chile & Garlic Dressing

Cut ¾ lb chicken breast into 1¼-inch pieces. Add 2 tablespoons light soy sauce, ½ tablespoon dark soy sauce, and 2 teaspoons ground black pepper.

Grind 2 garlic cloves and 2 seeded and chopped red chiles with a pinch of salt using a mortar and pestle until smooth. Add the leaves from 4 sprigs of cilantro and continue to grind to a paste.

Preheat the grill to hot. Thread the chicken onto soaked wooden skewers and grill it slowly, caramelizing on all sides for about 8 minutes, turning frequently.

Add the juice of 2 limes and 5 tablespoons warm water to the garlic paste and serve the sauce with the chicken skewers.

 Garlic Grilled Pork Chops

Crush 2 garlic cloves, 1 teaspoon coriander seeds, 1 teaspoon fennel seeds, 4 star anise, a pinch of salt, and a pinch of red pepper flakes using a mortar and pestle.

Rub the crushed mixture into 4 pork chops.

Preheat the grill to hot and grill the pork chops for 6 minutes on one side.

Turn the pork chops over and grill for 2 minutes, then remove from the heat and rest for about 2 minutes before serving.

Mix together a dressing of 1 tablespoon grated ginger, juice of 2 limes, ¼ teaspoon crushed white pepper, and 1 tablespoon fish sauce and pour this over the chops.

 Grilled Beef with Ginger & Coconut

Fry 1¾ oz flaked coconut, 1 tablespoon crushed coriander seeds, 1½-inch piece of peeled and grated ginger, and 1 seeded and chopped red chile over medium heat in a frying pan.

Cook slowly until the coconut and coriander are golden, toasted, and fragrant.

Grill 1 lb beef sirloin or rump until medium-rare and then let rest.

Tear the leaves from 3 sprigs each of cilantro and mint and add to the coconut.

Slice the beef thinly and add the juice of 1 lime and 1 tablespoon fish sauce.

Scatter over the coconut-mint garnish.

Braised Chicken
with rice, turmeric & spices

serves 4-6
• • • • • • • • •

preparation
15 minutes

cooking
15–18 minutes

This dish is essentially a pilaf where the chicken and rice are cooked together. It is a very easy dish to make and perfect for the whole family.

fresh

1 lb skinless boneless chicken thighs, cut into 1¼-inch cubes

2 garlic cloves, chopped

2 red chiles, seeded and finely chopped

3 cilantro roots, cleaned and chopped

1½-inch piece of ginger, peeled and grated

1 cup fresh chicken stock

3 spring onions, finely chopped

juice of 2 limes

2 mint sprigs, leaves picked

3 cilantro sprigs, leaves picked

spices

1 teaspoon *each* ground cinnamon, ground coriander, and ground turmeric

½ teaspoon ground cardamom

freshly ground black pepper

pantry

2 tablespoons vegetable oil

½ cup basmati rice

2 tablespoons light soy sauce

salt

1. Heat the vegetable oil in a heavy-bottomed pan over medium heat. Add the chicken and brown until golden brown, 4–5 minutes. Add the garlic, chiles, cilantro roots, and ginger and cook until fragrant, about 1 minute. Add the cinnamon, coriander, turmeric, cadamom, and some salt and pepper and cook for another minute, being careful that they do not burn.

2. Add the rice and stir together so that the spices start to coat the rice. Add the chicken stock and the soy sauce and cover with a lid. Simmer gently until the rice is cooked and all the liquid has been absorbed, 10–12 minutes.

3. Add the spring onions and lime juice and tear in the mint and cilantro leaves. Mix together and serve.

CHEF'S TIP

You can use fish or seafood here instead of chicken, but add the pieces of fish much later in the cooking process as they won't take as long to cook.

Thai Fried Rice

serves 4-6
● ● ● ● ● ● ● ● ●

preparation
10 minutes

cooking
10 minutes

This staple of Thai cuisine is a great way to use up leftovers, such as chicken satay, spice-roasted pork, shrimp, grilled fish, or vegetables.

fresh

1 yellow onion, finely chopped

3 garlic cloves, finely chopped

2 red chiles, seeded and finely chopped

2 skinless and boneless chicken breasts, sliced into ¼ inch slices

½ lb raw shrimp, peeled, cleaned, and halved lengthwise

2 eggs, beaten

5 cups cold cooked jasmine rice

juice of 2 limes

3 cilantro sprigs, leaves picked and roughly chopped

2 spring onions, finely chopped

spices

freshly ground black pepper

pantry

2 tablespoons vegetable oil

3 tablespoons fish sauce

1. Heat the vegetable oil in a wok over medium heat and fry the onion until softened, 1–2 minutes. Add the garlic and chiles and fry for another minute until fragrant and aromatic.

2. Add the sliced chicken and stir-fry briskly until the chicken starts to change color, then add the shrimp. Stir-fry briskly for 2 minutes, then add the eggs, cooking them on the upper edges of the pan so that you get a thin omelet.

3. Splash in the fish sauce, then add the rice and continue to stir-fry for 3 minutes. Season with black pepper and lime juice.

4. Add the cilantro and spring onions, then quickly transfer to a large serving dish.

CHEF'S TIP

Serve with Red or Green Nam Jim Sauce (pages 236–237), Hot & Sour Red Chile Sauce (page 234), or Peanut Dipping Sauce (page 242).

Braised Mushrooms
with ginger & chile

serves
• • • •

preparation
10 minutes

cooking
8–10 minutes

Mushrooms with ginger are a delicious combination. Serve this with some roasted meat, such as the Slow Roasted Pork Shoulder (page 104). You can use a mix of different cultivated and wild mushrooms in this dish if preferred.

fresh
3 cilantro roots, cleaned and finely chopped

1 red chile, seeded and finely chopped

2 garlic cloves, finely chopped

1½-inch piece of ginger, peeled and grated

1 lb oyster mushrooms, torn

¼ lb asparagus, cut into 1½-inch lengths

juice of 1 lime

2 cilantro sprigs, leaves picked and roughly torn

spices
½ teaspoon ground cinnamon

½ teaspoon five-spice powder

½ teaspoon ground coriander

freshly ground black pepper

pantry
2 tablespoons vegetable oil

salt

6 tablespoons rice wine

1 tablespoon light soy sauce

1 tablespoon toasted sesame seeds

1. In a medium bowl, mix together the cilantro roots, red chile, garlic, and ginger.

2. Heat the oil in a heavy-bottomed pan and sauté the garlic mixture until fragrant and aromatic.

3. Add the mushrooms and cook over high heat until the mushrooms begin to smell nutty and are beginning to caramelize and turn golden brown, 3–4 minutes.

4. Add the cinnamon, five-spice powder, and coriander and season well with salt and black pepper. Add the rice wine, soy sauce, and asparagus and cover with a lid. Simmer until all the liquid has been absorbed, about 4 minutes.

5. Add the lime juice, cilantro, and toasted sesame seeds. Mix together and taste and adjust the seasoning if needed. Serve right away.

serves
● ● ● ●

preparation
5 minutes

cooking
1 minute

Stir-fried Spinach
with garlic & black pepper

Cooking greens in a wok gives them an excellent smoky taste. Morning glory water spinach is a Thai variety that has a dark green blade-shaped leaf and a hollow stem and stir-fries in seconds. If not available, use baby spinach or a combination of spinach and other greens like Swiss chard or tender-stemmed broccoli.

fresh

3 small garlic cloves, finely chopped

1 red chile, seeded and finely chopped

1¼-inch piece of ginger, peeled and grated

1 lb fresh spinach (or Swiss chard or a combination)

juice of 1 lemon

spices

freshly ground black pepper

pantry

2 tablespoons vegetable oil

salt

2 tablespoons fish sauce

1. Heat the oil in a wok over medium heat, add the garlic, chile, and ginger and stir-fry until golden brown, about 30 seconds.

2. Add the spinach and stir-fry quickly over high heat, so they are coated in the oil, garlic, and chile.

3. Season with salt and lots of black pepper. Add the fish sauce and lemon juice, cook for another 30 seconds, and serve immediately. Serve as part of a meal with meat, fish, or rice dishes.

Stir-fried Mixed Greens
with oyster sauce

You can use any combination of green vegetables for this quick dish, such as tender-stemmed broccoli, green beans, or asparagus.

fresh

2 small garlic cloves, finely chopped

1 lb mixed green vegetables, such as tender-stemmed broccoli, green beans, asparagus, and sugar snap peas, trimmed to equal lengths

juice of 1 lemon

spices

pinch of red pepper flakes

freshly ground black pepper

pantry

2 tablespoons vegetable oil

2 tablespoons oyster sauce

salt

to serve

2 tablespoons toasted sesame seeds

3 cilantro sprigs, leaves picked

1. Heat the oil in a wok over medium heat, add the garlic, and stir-fry until golden brown, about 30 seconds. Add the mixed greens and a splash of water, raise the heat to high, and stir-fry for about 2 minutes longer.

2. Add the oyster sauce and pepper flakes and stir-fry for another 30 seconds so that they are coated. Season with salt and lots of black pepper. Add the lemon juice and serve immediately. Scatter over the toasted sesame seeds and cilantro leaves to garnish.

Desserts
& Drinks

chapter 7

Spiced Banana Fritters

serves 4-6
● ● ● ● ● ● ● ● ●

preparation
10 minutes

cooking
3 minutes
(per batch)

Banana fritters are a street-food staple stacked high in newspaper cones. They make a great snack, and there are lots of different variations, but I like this spicy one.

fresh

3 large unripe bananas (the skins just turning yellow)

spices

1 teaspoon ground cinnamon

½ teaspoon ground cardamom

¼ teaspoon ground nutmeg

¼ teaspoon ground cloves

pantry

⅔ cup all-purpose flour

½ cup rice flour

pinch of salt

1 tablespoon sesame seeds

1 cup coconut milk

2 tablespoons honey

vegetable oil, for deep-frying

1. In a large bowl, mix the flours with the salt, cinnamon, cardamom, nutmeg, cloves, and sesame seeds. Whisk in the coconut milk until you have a smooth batter. Add the honey and whisk until you have a batter that is the consistency of heavy cream.

2. Slice the bananas on the diagonal into 3–4 large slices, then cut each slice in half lengthwise so that you have strips about ⅜ inch thick.

3. Heat the oil for frying in a heavy-bottomed frying pan until a deep-frying thermometer registers 400°F or a cube of bread dropped in the oil browns in 15 seconds.

4. Dip the strips of banana in the batter, then shake off any excess. Fry in small batches until golden brown, about 3 minutes, then transfer to a paper towel–lined plate to drain. Serve immediately.

serves 8
• • • • • • • •

preparation
10 minutes

cooking
12 minutes

setting
40 minutes

fresh

1 package frozen young coconut
(find in the freezer section of
Asian markets), thawed, liquid
reserved and flesh shredded

grated zest of 1 orange

grated zest of 1 lemon

pantry

½ oz powdered agar agar
(or gelatin – either sheet or
powdered)

pinch of salt

1 cup superfine sugar

2 cups coconut cream

Thai Citrus &
Young Coconut Jelly

This is a striking-looking jelly because it has
two layers; one which is clear with citrus zest,
the other creamy with strips of coconut. Young
coconut is available frozen in its sweet water in
most Asian markets.

1. Put 3 cups water and 1 cup of the liquid from the package of
young coconut in a small saucepan. Stir in the agar agar powder (or
gelatin) and simmer for 10 minutes. Add the salt and sugar and stir
to dissolve. If using gelatin, follow the instructions on the package
for setting this amount of liquid.

2. Mix the shredded coconut with the coconut cream in another
saucepan. Add half the simmered sugar water and warm over a low
heat for about 2 minutes, but do not let it come to a boil. Let cool.

3. Add the orange and lemon zest to the remaining sugar water
and let cool (the orange will begin to color the liquid as it cools).
The liquid in both saucepans will start to set as they cool.

4. Pour the coconut cream mixture into 8 small, clean molds or
glasses, leaving enough space for the orange jelly. Let set in the
refrigerator for about 20 minutes.

5. Pour the orange jelly over the top of the set coconut cream and
let set in the refrigerator for 20 minutes. Serve with tropical fruits
such as mango, papaya, watermelon, or pineapple.

You could also make this layered
jelly in clear shot glasses, or in
a shallow dish, then cut it into
squares or diamond shapes.

serves 6
•••••

preparation
5 minutes

cooking
10 minutes

Sticky Rice
with mango

This is one of the most popular desserts in Thailand. The salt in the coconut cream is essential, because it brings out the flavor of the coconut rice.

fresh
1¾ cups cooked and still warm Thai Sticky Rice (page 248)

4 ripe mangoes

pantry
1 cup coconut milk

1 tablespoon granulated sugar

½ teaspoon salt

2 tablespoons coconut cream

1. Put the coconut milk and sugar in a medium saucepan and heat gently, stirring continuously to dissolve the sugar, being careful not to let the cream boil.

2. Add the salt and steamed rice and stir to combine. Set aside.

3. Cut the large cheeks off the mango as close to the center as possible, remove the skin, and cut the cheeks into 4 slices. Repeat with the other mangoes.

4. Place a mound of the warm rice in the center of each bowl and arrange the mango on top. Pour some coconut cream over the top and serve hot, warm, or cold.

Mango & Pineapple Salad

This fruit salad is a really refreshing end to a meal, particularly on a hot day. You can chill the salad slightly before serving it to get the full effect of its crisp textures.

fresh

20 mint leaves

1¼-inch piece of ginger, peeled

juice of 1 orange

2 ripe mangoes, peeled, pitted, and cut into large chunks

½ a pineapple, peeled and cut into half-moon slices (so they are a different size from the mango)

Mango sorbet (or other flavor), to serve

pantry

1 teaspoon superfine sugar

1. Using a mortar and pestle, grind the mint leaves, sugar, and ginger to a smooth paste. Add the orange juice and keep working the mixture until you have a smooth dressing.

2. Put the fruit in serving bowls, pour over the dressing, and gently mix together. Serve immediately with scoops of mango sorbet.

CHEF'S TIP

The key to making this zesty salad is buying good-quality ripe fruit. If fresh fruit is not available, make something else and wait until you have some prime sweet fruit.

preparation
5 minutes

cooking
10 minutes

Pineapple
with caramelized chile caramel

This is an amazing combination of flavors—the acidity of the pineapple offsets the sweet richness of the caramel.

fresh

2 red chiles, seeded and finely chopped

1½-inch piece of ginger, peeled and grated

3 long strips of orange zest

juice of 1 lime

1 pineapple, peeled, halved crosswise, and cut into ⅜ inch-thick slices

spices

3 cardamom pods, crushed

2 cinnamon sticks, snapped

3 star anise, broken

pantry

1 tablespoon vegetable oil

1¾ oz palm sugar, grated (or golden brown sugar)

1 tablespoon honey

1 teaspoon tamarind paste

pinch of salt

1. Heat a splash of oil in a frying pan over medium heat and fry the chiles, ginger, cardamom, cinnamon, star anise, and the orange zest until fragrant and aromatic, about 2 minutes. Add the palm sugar and honey and cook until caramelized, 3–4 minutes.

2. Add the tamarind paste, salt, and 4 tablespoons water and simmer until the mixture is sticky and caramelized and the consistency of honey, about 4 minutes.

3. Remove from the heat and add the lime juice. Taste to check the balance of flavors and adjust if needed.

4. Arrange the pineapple on a serving platter and pour the warm caramel over the top to serve.

serves 4-6
• • • • • • • • •

preparation
10 minutes

chilling
1 hour

Watermelon
with lime, salt & black pepper

This combination of flavors also works well as a refreshing drink – simply juice the watermelon, then add the other ingredients just before serving.

fresh

1 small watermelon, peeled
and cut into small pieces
(see box below)
juice of 2 limes

spices

freshly ground black pepper

pantry

salt

1. Put the watermelon pieces in the refrigerator for at least 1 hour to chill.

2. When ready to serve, add the lime juice to the watermelon and season well with plenty of black pepper and salt – do not be shy with the seasoning.

3. Mix together and taste to check the balance of flavors – make sure you can taste heat from the pepper, sweetness from the watermelon and salt and sourness from the lime juice – and adjust if necessary.

* how to *
SEED A WATERMELON

* *Use a sharp knife to cut off both ends of the watermelon and remove the skin, cutting from top to bottom, so that all the skin and the white areas of flesh have been cut away.*

* *Cut each half into wedges. If you view the melon wedge from the side, it is made up of three layers – the inside or core layer is smooth with no seeds. Remove this first inside layer with a small sharp knife, then cut into bite-size chunks.*

* *The second layer is where all the seeds are present. If you cut this into chunks every single one would have seeds in it, so use a sharp knife to remove all of this layer. This part of the melon can be used to make a delicious drink, so do not waste it. Instead, put all of the seeded section in a blender, then pour it through a sieve to strain out the seeds. Chill before serving.*

Toasted Coconut Ice Cream Topping

This delicious topping can be poured over vanilla ice cream to create a decadent dessert. It can also be used to scatter over a tropical fruit salad, pancakes, or oatmeal.

serves 4-6

● ● ● ● ● ● ● ● ●

preparation
10 minutes

cooking
7 minutes

fresh
1½-inch piece of ginger, peeled and grated

grated zest and juice of 1 orange

good-quality vanilla ice cream, to serve

spices
1 teaspoon ground cinnamon

½ teaspoon ground nutmeg

pantry
2 cups desiccated coconut

2 tablespoons honey

1. Put the coconut and ginger in a frying pan over medium heat and fry until fragrant and golden brown, about 3 minutes, keeping the pan moving so that the coconut does not burn.

2. When the coconut is just beginning to brown, add the cinnamon and nutmeg and cook for 1 minute so that they become aromatic and fragrant, but without burning.

3. In a small saucepan over medium-high heat, combine the honey and 2 tablespoons water and bring to a boil. Add the orange zest and simmer until the honey begins to caramelize, about 3 minutes. Keep moving the caramel around the pan until it develops a dark color, then remove it from the heat. Leave the caramel to turn as dark as brown sugar as it cools off the heat.

4. When the honey is dark and sticky, add the orange juice to stop the cooking.

5. Using a mortar and pestle, crush the spiced coconut.

6. Scoop some vanilla ice cream into serving bowls, pour over the burnt honey caramel, then scatter the spiced coconut over the top to serve.

Banana & Coconut Pancakes

serves 4-6
• • • • • • • •

preparation
15 minutes

cooking
2 minutes
(per pancake)

These pancakes are the perfect finale to a delicious meal of satay, fish cakes, and stir-fries that are packed full of flavors and fiery chiles.

fresh
2 eggs, beaten
4 large ripe bananas
lemon wedges, to serve

spices
1 teaspoon ground cinnamon, plus more for sprinkling

pantry
1 cup all-purpose flour
¾ cup rice flour
1 teaspoon baking powder
½ coconut milk
1 teaspoon golden brown sugar
pinch of salt
¾ cup desiccated coconut
vegetable oil, for cooking
confectioners' sugar, for sprinkling

1. Sift the flours, baking powder, and cinnamon into a bowl. Make a well in the center and add the beaten eggs and half the coconut milk. Mix well until you have a smooth batter, then stir in the remaining milk.

2. Peel the bananas and place in a separate bowl along with the sugar and salt. Mash with a fork, then add to the batter and stir together. Add the desiccated coconut and mix well.

3. Heat a frying pan over medium heat, grease with a little oil, then pour out any excess oil.

4. Fry a ladleful of pancake batter at a time for about 1 minute on each side until brown on both sides. Remove and repeat until all the batter is used up.

5. Sprinkle some confectioners' sugar on a sheet of parchment paper. Turn the pancakes out onto the sugar and sprinkle with a little confectioners' sugar and a pinch of ground cinnamon. Give them a squeeze of lemon juice, then fold into quarters and enjoy.

Pineapple, Lime & Mint Crush

serves 4-6

● ● ● ● ● ● ● ● ●

preparation
5 minutes

Serve as a refreshing drink on its own
or with a dash of vodka, tequila, or gin.

fresh

2 limes

½ a pineapple, peeled and cut
into chunks

3 mint sprigs, leaves picked,
plus more for garnish

1½-inch piece of ginger, peeled
and grated

1 glass full of ice cubes

spices

½ teaspoon freshly ground
black pepper

pantry

pinch of salt

1. Use a sharp knife to cut the skin and pith from the limes, then cut
the flesh into chunks.

2. Put all the ingredients in a food processor or blender and pulse
to form a pineapple crush, then serve immediately garnished with
mint leaves.

serves 4-6
● ● ● ● ● ● ● ● ●

preparation
5 minutes

cooking
12 minutes

Roasted Fruits
with Thai aromatic spices

Roasted fruits with spices is the perfect dessert –
it is rich and sophisticated, yet simple to make.
You can use any fruits for this, depending on
the season – apples, pears, quince, peaches,
nectarines and plums all work beautifully here.

fresh

6 pears, peeled and quartered

1½-inch piece of ginger, peeled
and grated

grated zest and juice of 2 oranges

1½ tablespoons butter, cut into
small pieces

spices

3 cardamom pods, crushed

4 star anise

3 cinnamon sticks

3 bay leaves

½ teaspoon freshly grated
nutmeg

½ teaspoon allspice

¼ teaspoon freshly ground
black pepper

pantry

1 tablespoon grated palm sugar

2 tablespoons honey

1. Preheat the oven to 350°F.

2. In a large bowl, mix together all the ingredients except for the
pears and butter. Add the pears and mix thoroughly so that the pear
pieces are well coated.

3. Pour the pears into a roasting pan in an even layer and top with
the pieces of butter; this will create a spiced butterscotch as it melts
with the honey.

4. Bake until the fruit has caramelized, about 12 minutes,
occasionally basting the fruit with the caramel during cooking.

Basics

chapter 8

Curry Pastes

There are numerous types of Thai curry pastes with the ingredients, quantities, and flavorings varying from region to region. They all follow the same basic method, so here is a selection of the most popular pastes to add to your repertoire.

Red Curry Paste

This is a classic red curry paste that can be used for many types of curry, from fish to shrimp to roasted duck.

serves 6
• • • • •

preparation
15 minutes

cooking
40 minutes

fresh

5 red chiles, seeded and finely chopped

2 lemongrass stalks, tough outer leaves removed and stalks chopped

1½-inch piece of ginger, peeled and finely chopped

4 garlic cloves

6 cilantro roots, cleaned and chopped

3 red onions, roughly chopped

1 red bell pepper, chopped

4 lime leaves

juice of 2 limes

spices

½ teaspoon ground white pepper

2 teaspoons ground turmeric

pantry

2 tablespoons vegetable oil

1 teaspoon shrimp paste (see page 18), roasted

1 teaspoon salt

2¾ cups coconut cream

2 tablespoons fish sauce

1. Preheat the oven to 400°F.

2. Mix all the fresh ingredients, except the lime leaves and lime juice, together in a bowl and add 1 tablespoon of the vegetable oil. Lay a piece of parchment paper on a baking sheet and spread out the mixed fresh ingredients on the tray.

3. Spoon the shrimp paste into one corner of the tray – it is very pungent when it is raw, but turns nutty and savory once roasted. Roast in the oven for 8 minutes until the ingredients are fragrant and aromatic and starting to caramelize.

4. Remove the tray from the oven, then place the roasted ingredients in a food processor or blender. Purée all the ingredients with the salt and white pepper until smooth. Start with the most fibrous and hard ingredients, so purée the lemongrass, ginger and cilantro roots first, then add the remaining roasted ingredients. Add 6 tablespoons water to loosen the paste.

5. To cook the paste, heat the remaining oil in a heavy-bottomed pan over medium-high heat. Cook the mixture slowly for about 20 minutes, stirring regularly to avoid sticking. Add the turmeric and lime leaves and cook for about 20 minutes until aromatic and fragrant. Add the coconut cream and simmer until reduced by half. Add the fish sauce and lime juice and mix through.

6. Divide the paste into 3 portions. It is now ready for other ingredients, such as meat, fish, or vegetables, to be added to it (see Red Curry with Chicken, page 156) or to be frozen for future use.

CHEF'S TIP

It's important to not add the turmeric to the food processor or blender as it will dye everything yellow. Only add the turmeric when you are cooking the paste.

Green Curry Paste

serves 6
• • • • •

preparation
15 minutes

cooking
35 minutes

The paste is the most time-consuming element of making a curry. Make a big batch of any of these delicious curry pastes, then keep them in the refrigerator or freezer in small batches until needed.

fresh
1½-inch piece of ginger, peeled and chopped
4 garlic cloves, peeled
4 lemongrass stalks, tough outer leaves removed and stalks chopped
6 cilantro roots, cleaned and chopped
2 small Spanish red onions
5 green chiles, seeded and chopped
3 lime leaves
juice of 1 lime

spices
1 teaspoon ground turmeric

pantry
1 teaspoon salt
1 tablespoon vegetable oil
1⅔ cups coconut cream
1 tablespoon fish sauce

1. Purée the ginger, garlic, lemongrass, and cilantro roots in a food processor or blender and pulse the ingredients until smooth. Add the salt to help break the ingredients down.

2. Add the onions and chiles and a splash of water and purée to a semi-smooth paste. In this raw state the paste can be kept in the refrigerator for 3–4 days in an airtight container.

3. Heat the oil in a heavy-bottomed pan. Add the puréed paste, ground turmeric and lime leaves and cook over a low-medium heat for about 20 minutes, stirring to prevent it from sticking, until aromatic.

4. Add the coconut cream and gently simmer for about 10 minutes until reduced by about one-third.

5. Add the lime juice and fish sauce and mix. At this stage the paste could be kept in the refrigerator for up to 1 week, or frozen in portion sizes.

6. Divide the paste into 3 portions. It is now ready for other ingredients, such as meat, fish, or vegetables, to be added to it (see Thai Green Curry with Shrimp, page 154) or to be frozen for future use.

Geng Gari Curry Paste

fresh

1¼-inch piece of ginger, peeled

4 red chiles, seeded

3 lemongrass stalks, tough outer leaves removed and stalks chopped

6 garlic cloves

3 red onions, chopped

juice of 2 limes

spices

1 teaspoon ground cumin

1 teaspoon ground coriander

1 teaspoon ground cinnamon

1 teaspoon ground nutmeg

1 teaspoon ground turmeric

pantry

1 teaspoon salt

1 tablespoon vegetable oil

2¾ cups coconut cream

1 tablespoon tamarind paste

2 tablespoons light soy sauce

1. In a food processor or blender, purée the ginger, chiles, lemongrass, garlic, and salt to a smooth paste. Add the onions and purée again. Add a little water to help bring it together to form a smooth paste.

2. Heat the oil in a heavy-bottomed pan over medium-high heat. Add the spices and cook for about 2 minutes until fragrant. Add the puréed paste and reduce the heat to low and cook slowly for 25–30 minutes, stirring frequently to prevent it from sticking, until aromatic.

3. Add the coconut cream and simmer for about 5 minutes until reduced by half. The cooked paste at this point can be kept in the refrigerator for 1 week or freezer for 3 months.

4. Add the lime juice, tamarind paste, and soy sauce, then taste to check the balance of flavors and adjust if needed.

5. Divide the paste into 3 portions. It is now ready for other ingredients, such as meat, fish, or vegetables, to be added to it (see Geng Gari Curry with Roasted Chicken, page 166) or to be frozen for future use.

A *geng gari* curry has a base of spices, such as cinnamon, cumin, and coriander, that are fried until aromatic before the rest of the paste is added. This gives the paste a great depth of flavor. It can be used for a vegetarian or meat curry.

serves 4-6

• • • • • • • • •

preparation
10 minutes

cooking
35–40 minutes

Hot & Sour Orange Curry Paste

fresh

4 lemongrass stalks, tough outer leaves removed and stalks finely chopped

6 cilantro roots, cleaned and finely chopped

1½-inch piece of ginger, peeled and finely chopped

5 red chiles, seeded and finely chopped

4 garlic cloves

2 red onions, roughly chopped

1 red bell pepper, roughly chopped

4 lime leaves

juice of 3 limes

spices

2 teaspoons ground turmeric

pantry

1 teaspoon salt

1 tablespoon vegetable oil

2¾ cups coconut cream

3 tablespoons tamarind paste

2 tablespoons fish sauce

1. In a food processor or blender, purée the lemongrass, cilantro roots, ginger, chiles, garlic, and salt to a smooth paste. Add the onions and bell pepper and purée again. Add a little water to help bring it together to form a smooth paste.

2. Heat the oil in a heavy-bottomed pan over medium-high heat. Add the puréed curry paste and cook the mixture slowly for 20–30 minutes, stirring regularly to prevent it from sticking. Add the turmeric and lime leaves and cook the paste for about 30 minutes over a low heat until aromatic.

3. Add the coconut cream and simmer for 5 minutes until reduced by half. Add the lime juice, tamarind paste and fish sauce, then taste to check the balance of flavors and adjust if needed.

4. Divide the paste into 3 portions. It is now ready for other ingredients, such as meat, fish, or vegetables, to be added to it (see Hot & Sour Orange Curry with Grilled Salmon, page 160) or to be frozen for future use.

This fantastic Royal Thai curry paste is a vibrant yellow-orange hue from the turmeric and is often used for a fish curry.

serves 4-6

● ● ● ● ● ● ● ●

preparation
10 minutes

cooking
1 hour

Mussaman Curry Paste
with roasted peanuts

A Mussaman curry is an amazingly delicious,
fragrant, and aromatic curry. It is similar to an
Indian curry and was brought to Thailand by
Muslim and Arab traders from Persia.

serves 8

•••••••

preparation
20 minutes

soaking
30 minutes

cooking
30 minutes

fresh

2 red onions, roughly chopped

6 garlic cloves, roughly chopped

2-inch piece of ginger or galangal, peeled and roughly chopped

4 cilantro roots, cleaned and chopped

3 lemongrass stalks, tough outer leaves removed and stalks roughly chopped

spices

3 long dried red chiles

2 teaspoons coriander seeds

1 teaspoon cumin seeds

4 cloves

½ teaspoon ground nutmeg

¾-inch cinnamon stick

4 green cardamom pods

pantry

½ cup blanched skinless peanuts

vegetable oil, for cooking

salt

1–2 tablespoons grated palm sugar

2 tablespoons fish sauce

2 tablespoons tamarind paste

6 tablespoons pineapple juice

1. Soak the dried chiles in boiling water for about 30 minutes until soft. When soft, remove the seeds and finely chop the flesh.

2. Toast the blanched skinless peanuts until golden brown. Place all the spices in a frying pan and toast until fragrant and aromatic, 3–4 minutes. Transfer to a mortar or spice grinder and grind to a medium-fine powder. Pour the ground spices through a sieve to separate any husks and woody bits.

3. Heat 1 tablespoon vegetable oil in a wok over medium-high heat and fry the chiles, onions, garlic, ginger, cilantro roots, and lemongrass for about 10 minutes until brown and fragrant. Add a little water if they are starting to stick.

4. Transfer to a food processor or blender and purée with the salt, spices, and the peanuts to a smooth paste.

5. Heat a heavy-bottomed pan over medium-high heat. Add a little oil, then cook the paste for about 10 minutes, stirring regularly to avoid sticking, until aromatic. Add add a splash of water if it begins to stick or burn.

6. When you can smell the spices, add the palm sugar and cook for about 5 minutes for it to caramelize.

7. Add the fish sauce and tamarind paste, stir in the pineapple juice and cook for another 5 minutes. Taste to check the balance of flavors and adjust if necessary.

8. Divide the paste into 3 portions. It is now ready for other ingredients, such as meat, fish, or vegetables, to be added to it (see Mussaman Curry with Spiced Braised Beef, page 162) or to be frozen for future use.

CHEF'S TIP

This paste can be used for a lamb, beef, or chicken curry and can be kept in the freezer for 3 months.

serves 4-6

preparation
5 minutes

marinating
1 hour

Spiced Marinade
for duck or chicken

Use this marinade on either a slow-roasted whole duck (like a Chinese-style roasted duck) or chicken, or on a duck or chicken breast cooked quickly on the grill.

fresh

2 garlic cloves, finely chopped

1½-inch piece of ginger, peeled and grated

4 cilantro roots, cleaned and finely chopped

juice of 1 orange

spices

1 teaspoon ground coriander

1 teaspoon ground cumin

1 teaspoon ground cardamom

pantry

1 tablespoon fish sauce

1 teaspoon palm sugar, grated

1 teaspoon ground black pepper

1. In a medium bowl, combine all the ingredients and stir well.

2. To use, in a shallow dish, pour the marinade over either a whole duck or chicken, or duck or chicken breasts, cover the dish with plastic wrap, and let marinate in the refrigerator for 1 hour before cooking.

Sauces

The sauces in Thai cooking are what really make the individual dishes sing, and they mark this cuisine as a tongue-tingling fireworks display. The balance of taste is very important, so taste the sauce before you serve it to be sure it suits your palate.

Thai Red Chile Vinegar

serves 4-6

preparation
5 minutes

This is a brilliantly addictive sauce and is great with grilled or roasted meat, particularly Spiced Bavette Steak (page 94).

fresh
2 long red chiles, seeded and finely chopped
1½-inch piece of ginger, peeled and grated
1 garlic clove, finely chopped
juice of 1 lime

pantry
¼ teaspoon salt
¼ teaspoon superfine sugar
2 tablespoons rice vinegar

1. Using a mortar and pestle, grind the chiles, ginger, garlic, salt, and sugar to a smooth paste.

2. Add the vinegar and lime juice and mix together. Add 3 tablespoons water to thin the sauce, and add a little more sugar if necessary. The sauce will keep for 1 week in the refrigerator.

Sang Wa

serves 4-6

• • • • • • • •

preparation
10 minutes

marinating
5 minutes

Sang Wa is a truly delicious
way of curing fish or shellfish.
It takes about 4 minutes to
cure thin slices of fish (see
variation below), and the
result is spectacular.

fresh

1 garlic clove

1½ red chiles, seeded and finely chopped

3 tablespoons orange juice

3 tablespoons lime juice

1½-inch piece of ginger, peeled and grated

1 lemongrass stalk, tough outer leaves removed
and stalk finely sliced

2 spring onions, finely sliced

3 lime leaves, stemmed and finely sliced

3 cilantro sprigs, leaves picked and finely sliced

pantry

½ teaspoon salt

½ teaspoon superfine sugar

1. Using a mortar and pestle, grind the garlic,
half the chiles, the salt, and sugar to a smooth
paste. Add the orange and lime juice and mix
to make a marinade.

2. Put the remaining ingredients in a bowl
and pour over the marinade. Let marinate for
5 minutes before using. The dressing will keep
for 2–3 days in the refrigerator.

Variation:

You can use Sang Wa to cure fish. Put 1 lb finely sliced white
fish fillets in a shallow dish. Pour over the dressing and leave
for 4–5 minutes to cure and marinate. The acidity will literally
cook the fish.

Hot & Sour
Red Chile Sauce

serves 4-6
● ● ● ● ● ● ● ● ●

preparation
5 minutes

cooking
2 minutes

This is a classic dipping sauce
that is packed full of flavor. Serve
with grilled shrimp or chicken,
as a dipping sauce with oysters,
or as a salad dressing.

fresh
1 garlic clove, finely chopped
¾-inch piece of ginger, peeled and finely chopped
2 long red chiles, seeded and finely chopped
juice of 2 limes

pantry
2 teaspoons rice vinegar
1 teaspoon superfine sugar
2 tablespoons fish sauce

1. Put ⅓ cup water in a small saucepan along
with the vinegar and sugar. Bring to a boil and
boil for 1 minute until the sugar has dissolved.
Let cool.

2. Stir in the garlic, ginger, and chile with the
vinegar and add the lime juice and fish sauce.
Taste to check the balance of flavors and adjust
if needed. The sauce will keep for 2–3 days in
the refrigerator.

Chile Tamarind Caramel Sauce

serves 4
●●●●

preparation
10 minutes

This is a delicious sauce combining all the elements of Thai cooking. It can be used on grilled fish, shrimp, chicken skewers, or as a salad dressing.

fresh
1½-inch piece of ginger, peeled and grated
2 red chiles, seeded and finely chopped
1 garlic clove, finely chopped
juice of 2 limes

pantry
1 tablespoon vegetable oil
1¾ oz palm sugar, grated (or golden brown sugar)
1 tablespoon honey
3½ tablespoons tamarind paste
2 tablespoons fish sauce

1. Heat a splash of oil in a pan over medium heat. Sauté the ginger, chiles, and garlic for about 2 minutes until fragrant and aromatic. Add the palm sugar and honey and cook for 3–4 minutes to slowly caramelize.

2. Add the tamarind paste, fish sauce, and 4 tablespoons water and simmer for about 5 minutes until sticky and caramelized.

3. Remove the pan from the heat and add the lime juice. Taste to check the balance of flavors and adjust if needed – it should be hot from the chile and ginger, sweet from the palm sugar and honey, sour from the tamarind and lime juice and salty from the fish sauce. The sauce will keep for about 1 week in the refrigerator.

Red Chile
Nam Jim Sauce

serves 4-6
• • • • • • • • •

preparation
10 minutes

fresh

2 garlic cloves
3 red chiles, seeded and finely chopped
3 cilantro roots, cleaned and chopped
juice of 1 orange
juice of 3 limes

pantry

½ teaspoon salt
1 teaspoon grated palm sugar
3 tablespoons fish sauce

1. Using a mortar and pestle, grind the garlic, chiles, and cilantro roots with the salt and sugar to a smooth paste. Add the orange juice, lime juice, and fish sauce.

2. Taste the sauce to check the balance of flavors and adjust if needed – the sauce should be hot from the chile, sweet from the orange and sugar, refreshingly acidic from the lime juice and salty from the fish sauce. This sauce will keep for 4–6 days in the refrigerator.

Green Chile
Nam Jim Sauce

serves 4-6
• • • • • • • • •

preparation
10 minutes

fresh

2 garlic cloves

3 cilantro roots, cleaned and chopped

4 long green chiles, seeded and finely chopped

3 cilantro sprigs, leaves picked

juice of 3 limes

pantry

1 teaspoon salt

1 teaspoon superfine sugar

2 tablespoons fish sauce

1. Using a mortar and pestle, grind the garlic
and cilantro roots to a smooth paste. Add the
green chiles, salt, and sugar and grind again.
Add the cilantro leaves and continue to grind
to a paste.

2. Add the lime juice and fish sauce. Add
¼ cup water to loosen the paste and dilute
the acidity. The sauce will keep for 4–5 days
in the refrigerator.

CHEF'S TIP

Serve grilled or spice-roasted
meat with the sauce splashed over
the top or as a dipping sauce.

Chiles

Chile releases endorphins and is addictive, so the more you eat, the better you feel and the more you crave. A good sweet chile sauce should have a balance of hot, sweet, salt, and sour. You could make a large quantity, put in sterilized jars, and give as a gift at Christmas. Chile jams or relishes are the perfect partner to many Thai dishes.

Sweet Chile Sauce

serves 4-6
● ● ● ● ● ● ● ● ●

preparation
10 minutes

cooking
12 minutes

fresh

½ lb red chiles, seeded
1½-inch piece of ginger, peeled and grated
4 garlic cloves

pantry

1 cup superfine sugar
1 tablespoon salt
6½ tablespoons rice vinegar

1. Put the red chiles, ginger, and garlic in a food processor or blender and blitz to a chunky paste.

2. Put the sugar, salt, vinegar, and 6 tablespoons water in a large heavy-bottomed saucepan and bring to a boil. Add the blended mixture and simmer for another 10 minutes.

3. Remove from the heat and set aside to cool. Pour into a sterilized jar and store for up to 2–3 weeks in the refrigerator.

Fresh Chile Jam

serves 4-6
• • • • • • • • • •

preparation
10 minutes

cooking
25 minutes

fresh
2 x 1½-inch pieces of ginger, peeled and grated
12 long red chiles, seeded and finely chopped
6 garlic cloves, peeled and chopped
6 cilantro roots and stems, washed and finely chopped
16 plum tomatoes
1 yellow onion, finely chopped
juice of 2 limes

spices
freshly ground black pepper

pantry
1 cup golden brown sugar
3 tablespoons fish sauce
2 tablespoons tamarind paste
salt

1. Put the ginger, chiles, garlic, and cilantro roots in a food processor or blender and pulse to a rough paste. Add half the tomatoes and the onion and pulse to a purée.

2. Transfer the purée to a pan and add the sugar, fish sauce, and tamarind and cook over medium heat for about 25 minutes until the purée starts to be syrupy and the liquid has reduced.

3. Cut the remaining tomatoes in half and remove the seeds. Cut the flesh into fine dice and add to the pan. Season well with salt and black pepper and add the lime juice. Taste to check the balance of flavors and adjust if necessary, then remove from the heat. As it cools, it will condense to a syrupy paste.

4. The jam will keep for 10–14 days in the refrigerator. However, I doubt that it will last that long and suspect that you will have eaten it before you need to worry about a used-by date.

CHEF'S TIP
Serve with almost anything—from scrambled eggs to grilled chicken—or use as a base for a sauce.

Nam Prik Pow Thai Chile Relish

preparation
15 minutes

cooking
1 hour

There are many different versions for chile (*prik*) relishes, pastes, and jams where the ingredients are either roasted or fried separately or cooked in a pan together to form these delicious condiments.

fresh

4 large red chiles, seeded and finely chopped

4 garlic cloves, chopped

1½-inch piece of ginger, peeled and chopped

3 onions, roughly chopped

juice of 2 limes

spices

¼ teaspoon crushed dried red chiles

2 teaspoons ground cinnamon

1 teaspoon ground coriander

pantry

3 tablespoons vegetable oil

2 tablespoons golden brown sugar

½ teaspoon salt

3 tablespoons tamarind paste

2 tablespoons fish sauce

1. Preheat the oven to 400°F.

2. Put the chile, garlic, ginger, and onions in a bowl with half the oil and mix together. Spread this mixture out in a roasting pan, then roast in the oven for 20 minutes until the onion and garlic are soft and starting to caramelize.

3. Transfer to a food processor or blender and add the brown sugar, salt, dried red chiles, cinnamon, and coriander and blend to a paste. Add the tamarind, fish sauce, and 6 tablespoons water and continue to blend to a smooth pulp.

4. Heat the remaining oil in a heavy-bottomed pan over medium-high heat. Transfer the puréed mixture to the pan, lower the heat, and cook for 40 minutes until the excess liquid has cooked away and the paste is turning to a jam-like consistency.

5. Add the lime juice and mix well. Taste to check the balance of flavors and adjust if needed. Pour into sterilized jars and store in the refrigerator for up to 1 month.

CHEF'S TIP Make a large batch, then store it in sterilized jars (like a jam or chutney) so that you can use it for anything from a beef stir-fry to a sandwich spread, or on eggs or vegetables.

preparation
10 minutes

cooking
10 minutes

Peanut Dipping Sauce

This is a delicious dipping sauce with lots of flavor and texture. You could serve it with any roasted or grilled meat, but it is especially good with the Salt & Spice Roasted Pork Belly (page 100).

fresh

3 cilantro roots, cleaned and finely chopped

1 garlic clove, finely chopped

1 red chile, seeded and finely chopped

4 shallots, finely chopped

juice of 1 lime

2 cilantro sprigs, leaves picked and chopped

pantry

freshly ground black pepper

to serve

salt

2 tablespoons light vegetable oil

2 teaspoons grated palm sugar

4 tablespoons blanched skinless peanuts, roasted

1 tablespoon light soy sauce

1. Using a mortar and pestle, grind the cilantro roots, garlic, and a pinch of salt until smooth. Add the red chile and shallots and continue to grind to a smooth paste.

2. Heat a heavy-bottomed pan over medium-high heat. Add half the oil and the spice paste and sauté for about 2 minutes until fragrant. Add the palm sugar and cook for 4 minutes until caramelized.

3. Add the roasted peanuts and continue to cook for 3–4 minutes until the peanuts are a deep golden brown. If the sugar begins to burn, add a splash of water.

4. Transfer the mixture back to the mortar and grind to a semi-smooth paste.

5. Stir in the remaining oil, the soy sauce, and lime juice. Add about 3 tablespoons water to thin the sauce and add the cilantro. Serve with crispy pork or chicken satay. This sauce will keep for about 1 week in the refrigerator.

Relishes & Pickles

Relishes and pickles are great with grilled or roasted meat such as the Slow Roast Pork Shoulder (page 104) or the Sweet & Crispy Pork Spare Ribs (page 110). They can accompany roasted chicken, grilled pork, or roasted duck and also work well with cooked shrimp.

Fresh Mango Relish

serves 4-6
• • • • • • • • •

preparation
5 minutes

cooking
12 minutes

fresh
2 ripe mangoes, peeled, pitted, and finely chopped
2 green chiles, seeded and finely chopped
juice of 1 lime

spices
½ teaspoon ground cumin
freshly ground black pepper

pantry
salt
1 tablespoon golden brown sugar
2 tablespoons tamarind paste

1. In a small saucepan, mix together all the ingredients, except for the lime juice, with 6 tablespoons water. Bring to a boil, then reduce the heat and simmer for 10 minutes or until the excess water has evaporated.

2. Remove from the heat and let cool. Stir in the lime juice. This relish will keep for 2–3 days in the refrigerator.

Fresh Fruit Pickle

serves 4-6
•••••••••

preparation
10 minutes

fresh

1 medium-hard pear (not too ripe), quartered, cored, and cut into ⅜-inch dice

1 hard (unripe) mango, peeled, pitted, and cut into ⅜-inch dice

1 crisp apple (such as Pink Lady or Braeburn), quartered, cored, and cut into ⅜-inch dice

juice of 1 lime

2 medium-hot red chiles, seeded and finely chopped

1 small onion, finely diced

1¼-inch piece of ginger, peeled and grated

spices

freshly ground black pepper

pantry

2 tablespoons rice vinegar

1 tablespoon grated palm sugar

salt

I. Mix all the ingredients together in a bowl and season well with salt and black pepper. Let stand for 5 minutes, then taste to check the balance of flavors and adjust if needed. This pickle will keep for a couple of days in the refrigerator; if it's stored any longer than that the fruit will become too soft and start to ferment.

Salt & Pepper Mix

serves 4-6

• • • • • • • • •

preparation
10 minutes

cooking
3 minutes

This is a fragrant and versatile dry spice mix that can be used for just about anything – it's particularly good on chicken, fish, or shellfish.

spices
1 tablespoon coriander seeds
2 teaspoons cumin seeds
2 teaspoons fennel seeds
5 whole star anise
½ teaspoon white peppercorns
½ teaspoon black peppercorns
1 teaspoon ground turmeric
pinch of red pepper flakes

pantry
3 tablespoons coarse salt flakes

1. Put all the ingredients, except for the salt, in a frying pan over medium heat and toast for 2–3 minutes, stirring constantly to keep the spices moving so that they do not burn, until fragrant and aromatic.

2. Transfer to a spice grinder or use a mortar and pestle and grind to a medium-fine powder – a little texture is fine but you do not want any big chunks of spices remaining.

3. Add the salt and stir together. This rub will keep well in an airtight container for a few weeks. Toast the mixture in a frying pan over medium-high heat to refresh the aromatic mixture before using.

CHEF'S TIP This is a handy mix to always have in your pantry. Use it to season meat, fish, shellfish, or steamed vegetables.

serves 4-6

• • • • • • • •

soaking
3 hours

steaming
30 minutes

Thai Sticky Rice

This is a broad, short-grained rice that becomes thick and glutinous when it is cooked. Use this rice for the classic Sticky Rice with Mango (page 204) and other fruit desserts.

fresh
1¼ cups uncooked Thai sticky rice (available at Asian markets)

1. Soak the rice in water for 3 hours, then drain and rinse thoroughly as it will be very starchy.

2. Set a steamer basket over a saucepan of water and lay a double layer of cheesecloth or muslin in the steamer. Pour the soaked rice on top.

3. Steam the rice over medium-high heat for 30 minutes until sticky and glutinous.

CHEF'S TIP

This rice must be manually steamed – it does not work well in an electric rice cooker.

Menu Planner

When you eat Thai food, you do not just have one dish; instead, you have a series of dishes that complement and contrast with each other. When planning a menu you have to think about the meal as a whole: what was eaten before and what will follow are important. There should be a balance of peppery hot, sweet, salt, and sour. This balance of taste should be present in every dish and across the whole meal. Some dishes are mild and others are spicy. Some dishes are smooth while others have more texture. One dish may be hot and salty while the next one is hot and sour. Color, taste, and texture are all important.

When preparing the ingredients, look at all the recipes for your meal and write a prep list. There may be ginger in a few dishes, so chop it once, then divide up the ginger for each dish. Lay out your prepped ingredients on a plate or cutting board like an artist's palette – chopped ginger next to sliced spring onions next to chile or garlic. If you follow this method it is easy to think about a meal with four or five components.

SATURDAY LUNCH: Tamarind Fried Shrimp (page 38), Grilled Pork & Herb Salad (page 92), Hot & Sour Orange Curry with Grilled Salmon (page 160), Toasted Coconut Ice Cream Topping (page 212), Pineapple, Lime & Mint Crush (page 216)

SIMPLE DINNER: Thai Beef Skewers with Red Chile Vinegar (page 88), Grilled Shrimp & Basil Salad (page 62), Chicken & Coconut Milk Soup (page 172), Pineapple with Caramelized Chile Caramel (page 208), Watermelon with Lime, Salt & Black Pepper (page 210)

FRIENDS COMING OVER: Crispy Chicken Spring Rolls (page 28), Crab & Lime Salad (page 74), Roasted Pork Shoulder with Coriander, Tamarind & Chile (page 104), Stir-fried Spinach (page 194), Mango & Pineapple Salad (page 206)

WANT TO IMPRESS: Cured Shrimp with Ginger & Lime Leaves (page 36), Roasted Duck Salad with Mango & Toasted Coconut (page 78), Turmeric Grilled Fish (page 130), Thai Green Curry with Shrimp (page 154), Banana & Coconut Pancakes (page 214)

MIDWEEK DINNER: Grilled Squid with Garlic & Pepper (page 40), Pork & Pickled Cucumber Salad (page 72), Sesame-seared Tuna with Lemongrass & Ginger (page 124), Pad Thai Fried Noodles (page 176), Toasted Coconut Ice Cream Topping (page 212)

FRIDAY NIGHT DINNER: Chicken Satay with Turmeric and Ginger (page 32), Crisp Cabbage & Cilantro Salad (page 66), Crispy Fried Whitebait with Thai Spices (page 126), Salt & Spice Roasted Pork Belly (page 100), Sticky Rice with Mango (page 204)

SOMETHING SPECIAL: Fried Crab Cakes with Cilantro (page 50), Sesame Chicken Salad with White Pepper (page 64), Coconut Fish Curry (page 152), Spicy Beef Noodles with Lime Leaves (page 180), Roasted Fruits with Thai Aromatic Spices (page 218)

Index

Acknowledgments

From Tom Kime:

I would like to thank all the chefs and food lovers who have inspired me over many years. This book is for you.

Thank you to both Katie Newton John and Maureen Miller for their generosity and patience having the team invade their beautiful homes and allowing us to shoot there.

I would like to thank Lisa Linder for her amazing photographs and Aya Nishimura and Ross Dobson for making my food look so delicious. A huge thank you to Catie Ziller, Abi Waters, and Alice Chadwick for bringing this great project to life.

Thank you to my wife Kylie, for her tireless support and all the great things we share. I love you.

Thank you to my boys Alexander and Orlando, for being such enthusiastic eaters and making meal times such a highlight of our day.

To my sister Hannah, for being so courageous. I hope you enjoy using this book, I thought of you when I was writing it.

Thank you to my dad Robert, for teaching me how to look at things and appreciate what is good.

To my mum Helen, who gave her love to people through her amazing food and taught me the love of cooking.

Thank you.

From Lisa Linder:

A big thank you to Tammy, Jim, and Rebecca for kindly putting us up and helping us enormously throughout the shoot. And Amelia Wasiliev for driving miles with her gorgeous props always with a big smile :-).

And the lovely Chaz for giving up her time and modeling for us so beautifully.

TOM KIME has worked in some of the best restaurants in London and Sydney. He has travelled extensively to discover and sample the world's best street food. Having cut his catering teeth with Rick Stein, Tom has worked at the River Café alongside Jamie Oliver (he cooked at Jamie's wedding) and at Darley St Thai with David Thompson. His first book, *Exploring Taste and Flavor*, published in 2005, (now retitled *Tasting*) won a World Gourmand Award. The 2007 World Gourmand Awards presented a silver medal to his second book, *Street Food*. In 2015, *Fish Tales*, Tom's fifth book, was honored by the World Gourmand Awards as one of their "best of the best books from the last 20 years." Tom has also hosted three of his own television series and filmed five series of the popular Australian series *Ready Steady Cook*. From 2010 to 2015 he was the Executive Chef at Fish & Co., the sustainable seafood café in Sydney. Most recently, Tom joined GoodTime hospitality in Sydney as the Group Executive Head Chef. He works as an international food consultant, writer, and presenter.

weldon**owen**

Published in North America by Weldon Owen
1045 Sansome Street, Suite 100
San Francisco, CA 94111
www.weldonowen.com

Weldon Owen is a division of Bonnier Publishing USA.

Copyright © 2017 by Hachette Livre, Département Marabout

Originally published in French as *Mon Livre de Cuisine Thaïe*

Library of Congress Cataloging-in-Publication data is available

ISBN: 978-168188-302-1

This edition printed in 2017
10 9 8 7 6 5 4 3 2 1

Printed and bound in China

Photographer: Lisa Linder
Illustrations: Alice Chadwick